MY REAL ESTATE NIGHTMARE

(based on a true story which means it happened
more or less like this
... but with uglier people.)

By Bob Boog

OTHER BOOKS BY BOB BOOG

Selling Outside the Square – (if you like *My Real Estate Nightmare* , you might like *Selling Outside the Square* too)

Acknowledgments

To my wife, **Roxana**, thank you for being in my life. Te quierro mucho! To my sons, **Brandon** and **Kevin**, you are never too old to keep chasing your dreams.

To my best friend, rock, and right-hand man, **Jim Behan**, thank you for your help, humor, friendship and support. Your kind Christian actions speak louder than words.

Thank you to my **Facebook friends**☺ Ralph Gibbs, Cyndi Conley, Sharon Valentine Rex,Cathy Earl Saltee, Heidi Steinmann Sankey, Carol Perralta, John Dalton, Jehane Lopez, Gabriela Walker,Wendy Gentile-Moliere, Judy Boog-Fiebelkorn, Joni Cluff Solis, Susan Vann, Cindy Clark Dean, Richard A. Patterson and Katya Savina.

Although this book is based on a true story, it is a work of fiction, which means some of this happened, and some of this didn't. What this also means to you, I am not offering any legal, tax or real estate advice and that I steal jokes from the Internet and my friend Google. Names of people, real, dead or imagined have been changed to protect their true identities.

CONTENTS

-0-

PROLOGUE

I'm not really a doctor, but I play one at Starbucks.

My name is Bob Boog and I am the author of this book and a real estate broker and owner of a small company called Bob Boog Realty. If you are wondering, I pronounce my last name like "Boogie-man" and not with a long O sound like a "bow" although a friend from Europe told me that "boog" means "bow" or "arch" in Dutch.

My realty company is located in Santa Clarita, California and for those of you unfamiliar with Southern California, Santa Clarita lies about 33 miles north of downtown Los Angeles, or 35 miles east of the Pacific Ocean and about 100 miles away from the mountains where in the winter there is skiing or snowboarding. There is a popular 262 acre theme park called Six Flags Magic Mountain planted four miles away from Santa Clarita so a lot of people know where that is.

People in real estate will often use minutes instead of miles to help sell our location which I think borders on being a little deceptive. We will tell a house-hunter, for example, "Santa Clarita lies only 34 minutes from the beach without traffic" or "Santa Clarita is just 30 minutes north of downtown LA, without traffic". This sounds pretty appealing, doesn't it? But who is kidding who? Because in Los Angeles, there is almost ALWAYS traffic.

A person could drive to LAX (Los Angeles International airport) at 2:00 in the morning on a Sunday and STILL probably hit traffic. Thank goodness for those wide, paved road shoulders that important people like me are entitled to use during traffic jams.

Actually, I am not that important because I am a middle child. I am the fifth child in a family of nine children. I have four older siblings and four younger, so what this means to you, is that I am a skillful negotiator. I have been bargaining since I have been in diapers!

I was born in St. Paul, Minnesota and I could not walk until I was about four years old. This is a true thing. I would either crawl or roll to where I wanted to go. I could stand up but then I would just fall down. A doctor told my mother that I might not ever walk because my knees and ankles were too weak, so my mom strapped my older sister's ice skates to my little feet and took me ice skating on a frozen lake. Mom told me that eventually I became strong enough to let go of her hand. She bragged that I could ice skate before I learned how to walk and was big enough to wear those braces like Forrest Gump. Nowadays, I am a little bowlegged but I'm not even pigeon-toed! Amazing, isn't it? However, we will not mention the damage that all those face-first head plants on the frozen ice did to my undeveloped brain, will we?

But that's enough about me. Let's get started with this nightmare!

Bob Boog

nightmare
[nahyt-mair]

1. A terrifying dream in which the dreamer experiences feelings of helplessness, extreme anxiety, sorrow, etc.

2. A condition, thought, or experience suggestive of a nightmare: the nightmare of his years in prison.

3. (Formerly) A monster or evil spirit believed to oppress persons during sleep.

-1-

PASTOR JIM

There is a sign hanging above the door of the one-story house which reads: "Pastor Jim – Christian Counselor" and after I had knocked a few times the door finally swung open. The person standing before me was a good-looking 65 year old man, standing about 6'1 tall and weighing 210 lbs. A thick patch of white hair had been parted to one side and he wore a big smile on his tanned face. His shirt had wet under-arms and he reminded me of a used car salesman.

"Pastor Jim," I introduced myself, "Bob Boog." He shook my hand firmly.

"Pleased to meet you, Mr. Boog. Do you want to come in? Or would you prefer that we chat in your car?"

"My car," I suggested. "We have a good half hour ride to Agua Dulce with traffic."

Pastor Jim followed me to my late-model Honda Pilot and got in. I started up the car and pulled away. Neither of us said anything of substance until we got onto the freeway, then

Pastor Jim started:

"On the phone you mentioned Christian counseling, but can you tell me a little bit more about what it is exactly that you want me to do?" he asked.

"Yeah, sure. You were Kelly Mere's youth minister, am I right?"

"Youth pastor," he corrected.

"Minister, pastor, whatever. Here's the thing. Six months ago, I sold Kelly a house on five acres in Agua Dulce. It was built like a duplex so two families could live there. She paid $126,000 for it cash and spent another $25,000 to fix it up. When I saw the beautiful job she did, I suggested that I could sell it for $250,000. So she listed the house with me."

"Well!" Pastor Jim boomed. "That's quite a return on investment."

"Right. But as soon as I got back to my office, she changed her mind and decided to rent out the house. She asked me if I could help her rent it and I said 'Sure.' The problem is, however, that the house is shaped like a big horseshoe, with a kitchen, bathroom, and 2 bedrooms on each side."

"So? Does that matter?" he asked.

"The problem is that Kelly still wanted to live there. Whenever I showed the house to prospective tenants, she would introduce herself and most people thought it was kind of creepy to have the landlord living right next to them."

"I see. So what happened?"

I glanced at him. "Kelly ended up finding the tenants but she asked me to check out their credit, so I did. That's all I did."

"And how was their credit?"

"These folks had the worst credit I have ever seen. So, even though I had advised her NOT to rent the house to them, a few days before Christmas, they showed up at my office. Kelly asked me to draw up rental agreements for them."

"So Kelly changed her mind."

I briefly lowered my head and checked the rear view mirror before answering.

"Exactly. She told me these people were good Christians that she had met at church but they had no place to go and had to be out of their place before Christmas. I told her NOT to rent to them, but then Kelly asked me if I was a Christian."

"Are you?"

"No, not really. I mean, I'm spiritual, but I really don't consider myself to be a Christian."

"Ahh, I see."

"Exactly, she took things the wrong way. And I told her this is not about religion. This is business. And business is business, right? Not renting to people three days before Christmas has nothing to do with my religion, or lack of it, as the case may be."

"Then what happened?"

"A few days before Christmas, John and Debbie Curston, that's their names, showed up at my office and asked for the keys to Kelly's place. I said, 'Keys! She is not renting to you.' They told me, 'Yes she is. We made a deal with Kelly last night and everyone was supposed to meet at Bob Boog's office at 9:30 in the morning.' Then about two minutes later, Kelly showed up."

Pastor Jim looked at me. "So, Kelly had made a secret agreement to rent the house to them."

I thought back to that day. Kelly was a slender attractive blond with perfect teeth, tanned skin and large blue eyes. She had a soft spot for animals and made it her mission to rescue as many kitty-cats as she could, all of whom were loved and nurtured in her care. Fond of riding horses, Kelly was an excellent horsewoman and once competed in barrel riding at rodeos. She usually wore flannel shirts, jeans and boots and had her hair in a pony tail. Kelly had a certain disaffected ease or innocence about her as do many women who are unaware of their striking good looks.

Pastor Jim looked at me and repeated. "So Kelly had made a secret agreement?"

"Yes, yes exactly. Kelly said to me again, 'Should I rent to them?' Finally I told her 'Look, it's your house, not mine. You can rent it to whomever you want.'"

Pastor Jim turned and eyed me carefully. "Kelly is 45 years old, isn't she?"

"Right. She's a big girl now, so I advised her to make it a month-to-month agreement. If things didn't work out, Kelly could kick them out in 30 days. The Curstons piped up. They claimed that Kelly had agreed to give them a one year lease, and so Kelly met them in the middle. She had me write up a six month term, from January 1st through June 30th. I drew it up as a favor to her, but I made it clear that I wanted nothing to do with the Curstons. I did not charge her a penny for my services. This was her doing, not mine."

"And what did Kelly say to that?"

"She was fine with it. Now, to understand the situation completely, you have to realize that both John and Debbie Curston are the type of people that when you look up 'trailer trash' in the dictionary, their faces would show up."

"That bad, eh?" he said.

"Well, let me put it like this: you know how they show subtitles during the TV show *Here Comes Honey Boo Boo*? I mean, the TV station has got to be laughing thinking that anyone watching might actually know how to read, right? In other words, the Curstons would fit right on that show."

Pastor Jim didn't crack a smile. He just shook his head.

"I still don't know what you want me to do," he said.

"I'll get to that. At first Kelly was thrilled with the arrangement. In fact, after the Curstons moved in, she called, telling me how happy she was, and that she finally had someone that she could talk to."

I took a swig of water from a plastic Arrowhead water bottle, and continued.

"The problem is that once she moved in, Mrs. Curston realized that Kelly Mere can talk your ear off. And it didn't take long for Debbie Curston to realize that she didn't really want to listen to Kelly. In fact, she wanted nothing to do with her. So, two weeks later, Kelly called me and asked, 'If I move out of my side of the house, could you please rent it for me?' And I said, 'Sure, no problem.' And she insisted that I sign a property management form and fax it to her, so I did. So there is a property management agreement form with my signature on it."

"And now Mrs. Curston is not talking with Kelly," said Pastor Jim.

"Exactly, but before Kelly moved out, the two of them got into some kind of a physical altercation."

"A fist-fight?"

"Not exactly," I explained. "Apparently Kelly picked up a metal pipe and, in a fit of rage, struck Debbie Curston with it."

"Oh my God. This gets stranger by the minute."

"It gets worse. So the Curstons called the police who went out to the property and arrested Kelly. Then the Curstons filed a restraining order and a judge ruled in their favor to have it enforced against Kelly."

Pastor Jim looked at me. "Do you blame them?"

"I don't know what to think," I said. "So now Kelly is unable to be within 100 yards of her own residence. And of course, the Curstons stopped paying the rent. Do you see what a fine mess this is?"

"Well, I can see they have their differences. But what is it you want me to do?"

"After this happened, Kelly called me. She said, 'I want you to sell the house' and, believe it or not, I was able to do it. I sold the house and we closed escrow on April 15th."

"Good job. So, Kelly is no longer the owner?"

"Right," I agreed, "but she is not out of the woods yet. See, in order to close escrow with the tenants still in possession of the property, Kelly signed a counter offer where she agreed to evict the Curstons as well as pay the buyer's new monthly payment. So each month that the Curstons stay there, they are costing Kelly money. And that's where you come in."

"Me?" he asked.

"Yes, you. Because you are a Christian. They met at church and they are both Christians. You can remind the Curstons that they are Christians. And staying there without paying rent for several months is not a Christian thing to do, right?"

"You couldn't do this?" Pastor Jim asked me.

"Me? No, not me. The Curstons don't like me, but you can do it because you are a minister."

"Well, I'm not a minister. I am Kelly's former youth pastor."

"Whatever," I said again.

"My dear Bob, you must realize that this situation is really about you."

"Me?" I looked over at him like he was critiquing my driving. "I don't think so. Anyway, I am not finished."

"Go on," he said calmly.

"The other problem we had was this: we sold the house to a Mexican family for $248,000. However, the appraisal of the house came in at only $224,000, so we were short by $24,000. So I suggested to Kelly, 'Why not sell your pony to the buyer for $24,000?'"

"Pony? Why a pony?"

"Kelly told me that she had paid $500 bucks for this pony, and we needed something of value that we could use to secure a note against. And some horses are worth millions of dollars, right?"

"Some thoroughbreds perhaps," Pastor Jim agreed, "but why not just use the property as collateral?"

"We couldn't. Things changed after the mortgage meltdown and the buyer was on a special program that was running out, so we had two weeks from the time the appraisal came back to close the sale. We had to use something, and the buyer's ten year-old daughter loved that pony. She would feed it apples and carrots every time they came out to see the property. It made perfect sense."

"So, did the buyer agree to pay $24,000 for the pony?"

"Yes. The buyers agreed to make monthly installments on it. But now that Kelly has been kicked out of the property, the pony is still there and I am concerned that the Curstons might not be feeding it."

"Bob, there is one thing that you don't understand."

"Yes?" I looked over at him.

"No Christian is ever going to allow a pony to die."

"No good Christian," I corrected. "These people are not good Christians. These are people who think that hating other people who are not Christians, like me, makes them good Christians."

"I doubt that," he said confidently.

"Well, wait until you meet these people," I muttered under my breath and I thought back to a few months earlier when I had served the Curstons with eviction papers.

-2-

EVICTION PAPERS

The tiny town of Agua Dulce is situated 20 miles east of Santa Clarita or about ten minutes without traffic, right? From January through March, this rocky, mountainous area turns a beautiful green. However, for the rest of the year the rocky hillsides spotted with green scrub oak trees dry out and become browner than a cardboard box. Agua Dulce is semi-famous, because they filmed *The Flintstones* movie here. The name means "Sweet Water" in Spanish and because there is no public water system, most of the houses in this area sit on five acre parcels with private water wells and septic systems.

The last time I had visited the Curstons' house, I had gone there alone. I had agreed to deliver the unlawful detainer action papers for Kelly's eviction attorney because several attempts to do so had failed.

First, Kelly's eviction attorney had tried to serve the Curstons by mail, but Mr. and Mrs. Curston were old pros at the eviction game. They didn't use an Agua Dulce physical address for their mail. They collected their mail via a post office box and therefore all packages sent to them at the house just got returned to the sender. Then her eviction attorney hired a process server who claimed he could not locate the address. Finally, the last process server failed, because he stated he had "feared for his life."

This process server claimed that Mr. Curston had told him, "I have a loaded shotgun and if you open my gate I will blast your head to kingdom come."

Yet, when Kelly's eviction attorney asked me if I would be willing to serve the papers, I said, "Sure, why not?" I was confident that Mr. Curston would not fire at me. After all, I wasn't just some stranger walking onto his property.

Looking back, I don't know why I felt so secure, but I did.

That day, with the eviction papers firmly in one hand and my iPhone in the other (to record the event via the video recorder of my smart phone), I stepped towards the horseshoe-shaped house. A chain link fence ran across the entire five-acres with a wrought-iron gate about 20 feet away from the front door. There was a row of oleander bushes hiding the house from public view.

I had just swung open the wrought iron gate only to be met by Billy Curston: 26, a young, angry-looking thug. Billy resembled a younger Brad Pitt with his long, dirty blond hair and his semi-handsome face wore a constant scowl. He had on jeans but no shirt, which revealed a muscular body tatted up with prison tattoos with swastikas and Aryan Nation crap. His breath reeked of alcohol, too.

"What the hell do you think you're doing?" he yelled at me. He looked about as happy as a rattlesnake who has just gotten kicked in the head.

"Don't kill me, I'm just the messenger." I tried to sound friendly yet nonchalant but I could tell that Billy was not buying it. "I just have to post this notice on the front door and then I'll be out of your hair."

He suddenly swung a fist at the papers which caused them to fall out of my hand and drop to the ground.

I held out my cell phone, steadying it with both hands, focusing it on his angry face.

"Is that your little celly phone?" he said in a sing-song voice. He pronounced "celly" so it sounded almost like "silly".

I nodded. "Yep."

He started to laugh and then stopped. "What are you gonna do with that little celly phone? Gonna call your momma?"

I have to admit, at this point, I was a little nervous, but I was dumb enough not to show it.

"Actually, I'm taking a video right now," I explained. "You see, with these smart phones, one push of a button and my video goes straight to the police department and puts you back in prison or back under that rock or hole you climbed out from under."

As I said this, a shapely woman in her mid 20's emerged from the house. She had a cigarette in one hand and a glass of bourbon in the other. She had on a peasant blouse, short-shorts and shoes where the high-heels are made of clear plastic. Two words immediately came to mind: stripper mom.

She sprinted to Billy's side and wrapped her arms around him, trying to pull him away from me, revealing a decent amount of cleavage too, I might add.

"A video?" Billy questioned defiantly.

"Yep, it records your voice too."

"You're a liar!" he sneered. "You can't take no video with a cell phone."

"Billy, that's one of them new-fangled things, it's called an eye-phone." she warned, brushing her blond hair from her eyes. "They can take videos with them things, that's how they nailed Monica at the pawnshop. Now, get back in the house. Let me handle this."

"No."

"Billy, let me handle this!" she said firmly. "You wanna go back? Do you wanna go back? Do you? I'm serious. You don't know them new-fangled things nowadays. They is smart."

Bill had a deranged look in his eyes like he was thinking, 'Dear schizophrenia, I don't understand English very well, so please speak slowly.' Finally, Billy snapped back to reality and stomped back to the house.

I watched as he angrily slammed the door. I waited till I was sure he was inside before I bent down to pick up the eviction papers from the ground. Whew!

I gazed up at stripper mom. "Hey, I'm just doing my job."

"I know who you are," she said. "Your name is Bob Boog. You're the one who got us into this effing mess in the first place!"

Me? I thought. I am being blamed for them being evicted? They think it's MY fault that Kelly rented the house to THEM? I didn't want them here in the first place. I shook my head in disbelief.

"What's your name?" I asked.

She took a long drag from her cigarette before answering. "Cynthia."

"What are you doing over there Cynthia?" I said. "That's Kelly's side of the house, isn't it?"

"Not any more," she explained. "Now please, don't cause us no problems, Billy just got out of state." She flicked ashes from the end of her cigarette more often than necessary, flipping her thumbnail against the filter.

"Look, as far as I know, you're trespassing because you are not on the lease," I said. "Just your mom and dad are. I wrote up their rental agreement."

"Well, Kelly signed a NEW contract with me, last night."

"Really?" I said. "Let me see it."

"Wait here and I'll fetch it."

While she went to retrieve the rental agreement, I taped the "Unlawful Detainer" papers to the front door. I made a smiley face on it for good measure. Then I switched my cell phone from video mode to camera mode and clicked a few pictures of the papers hanging from the front door.

Once that was done, I started back towards my car and tried to get my heart to slow down because Billy had come outside again. He clenched his jaw and was standing at Cynthia's side, gnashing his teeth.

"Here is our contract." She handed me a sheet of yellow-lined paper with some handwritten sentences scribbled on it. I could instantly tell that Kelly's left-handed signature had been forged, so I turned my back to them, snapped a picture of the document, and then returned it to her.

"Okay, looks legit to me," I sang and I headed back to my car.

"Hey, ass-wipe," Billy called. "You ain't never gonna kick us out of here! We're gonna burn this piece of shit down before we move out. And we're gonna barbeque that fucking pony too!"

I grinned and tried to give him the best impression of my teenage son. I rolled my eyes and chewed my gum as if to say, "Whatever."

"Hey, shit for brains!" he yelled loudly. "Can you believe that asshole?" he told Cynthia. "He's walking away from me. Hey, I'm talking to you," I heard Billy scream. "I'm talking to you!"

Loser, I thought as I got in my car and I tore out of there, pretending to be as ignorant as a hillbilly.

****

"That was my last meeting with the Curstons," I told Pastor Jim. He seemed perplexed.

"I still don't understand why you got so involved. Kelly is no longer the owner of the property, correct? Why don't you just let the new owner handle all of this?" he advised.

"Easy. Because if I do, the new owner is going to hire a lawyer and sue me," I explained. "And I have never been sued before. So I am doing my best to avoid being sued by the buyer. After all, they agreed to close escrow with the tenants in possession as long as Kelly paid to remove the tenants. But Kelly legally can't do anything because the tenants filed a restraining order against her. That's why I am doing this."

"Okay, again, what is it exactly, that you want me to do?"

"I want you to talk to them," I said. "Get them to forgive Kelly and move out. Tell them Kelly deserves to be forgiven because you all are Christians, and Christians forgive people, right? After all, didn't John say, 'Since God so loved us, we also ought to love one another?'"

Pastor Jim failed to respond.

"Well that's what Christians always tell me," I said. "Christians forgive one another, right? That and Christian Mingle, where God has hidden the perfect match for you on a website." Secretly I've always thought that Christian Mingle sounded like a product by Kraft but I didn't say this aloud.

He didn't utter a peep.

I exited the freeway at Red Rover Mine Road and headed south a mile or two and then turned left on a dusty dirt road.

I pulled up to the front of the house and stopped the car.

Our doors swung open simultaneously as we both got out. I stepped towards the residence. A prominent "No Trespassing" sign had been posted on the front gate, so I rattled it.

From inside the house, we could hear a dog bark. Finally, the front door opened and "stripper mom" Cynthia appeared. She was barefoot and wearing a halter top without a bra underneath and cut-off jeans. A vision of a foul-mouthed Ellie Mae from the Beverly Hillbillies flashed in my head. She had a cigarette in one hand and a can of Coors Lite in the other.

She stepped towards us. "What the hell do you want?" she yelled. She turned her head to blow out a puff of smoke and acted as if she would rather not look at me.

"This is Pastor Jim," I introduced. "He is a Christian. He wants to ask you something."

"I'm not talking to you, piece of shit," she spat back at me. Any person with eyes in their head could see that she was not happy with me.

I ignored her. "Pastor Jim, meet Cynthia. Cynthia here is a fine Christian woman."

"Cynthia, it is my pleasure to meet with you today," said Pastor Jim.

"I don't want him around here," she pointed at me with her cigarette. Her voice raised up an octave or two. "Do you know what happened to my husband last night? The police came out here and dragged him off again in handcuffs. And, it was all because of you."

She glared at me accusingly.

"Me?" I said. "What did I do?"

"My husband picked a fight with a man he thought was you; the neighbor."

"Jesus" I said. "Is he okay?"

"Who cares about him? But who did the police put in jail? Not the son-of-a-bitch who beat my husband to a bloody pulp. My husband!" she wailed, "My poor husband is back in jail!"

"I'm sorry to hear that," I said, not feeling sorry at all. I had my cell phone in my hand and clicked the video capture button. After all, good redneck humor is hard to come by but I was nonchalant about it too and just held my iPhone near my ear like I was trying to hear something while keeping eye contact with her.

She stopped as if she had a sudden thought. "You know, it must suck to be you," she continued, "I mean I actually feel sorry for you because it must really suck to be Bob Boog."

She moved closer to Pastor Jim and pointed at me. "Did you know that he had no business with finding us this place? We struck a deal with the owner ourselves, but then Mr. Bob

Boog here had to go and mess the whole thing up. My mother would have owned this place if it wasn't for that man."

She seemed very sincere. And I almost wanted to laugh out loud, but didn't because I kept thinking how I was going to upload this video to YouTube and share it with all my friends. This was becoming an instant classic! I kept a serious face though as I nonchalantly continued filming.

"Yeah, well, I bet a lot of people feel the same way," I joked. I had tried to sound cute for the camera, but I knew I had said the wrong thing because she looked at me like she smelled microwaved curry chicken stuffed with burnt popcorn.

"You-- you Satan worshiper! I hate you!" she screamed. "I fucking hate you! You, Bob Boog, you, worthless piece of shit!"

"Cynthia, Cynthia calm down, please." Pastor Jim reminded me of a landed fish gasping in shock yet doing his best to calm her down but I could see that she was now a mental mess.

"What the fuck is wrong with you?" she said to Pastor Jim while pointing her entire arm at me. Her eyes, a mess of melted liner, showed the evidence of her tears. "That man there is the devil. Can't you fucking see that? That Bob Boog, sold this house under our fucking noses. We would have owned this place if it weren't for him!"

"Well, Christ taught us that we must learn to forgive our enemies, didn't he? Jesus said, 'Your strong love for each other will prove to the world that you are my disciples.'"

There was a pregnant, awkward pause where I thought that perhaps his words had gotten through to her.

"Oh, fuck off!" she spat, "Both of you—Now! Or I'm calling the cops! You! You! Bob Boog, you should be in jail. Not my husband!"

Pastor Jim looked over at me. "I think it's time for us to leave."

"You think?" I joked.

I clicked off my video camera as I stepped towards my car and as we did, the sound of loud music began to play from a boombox that Cynthia had brought outside.

The song was *Jesus Take the Wheel* by Carrie Underwood. It was obviously deeply meaningful to Cynthia, but it struck me as being ironic.

I started thinking to myself how no car insurance company would ever back a claim if you told them that you had allowed Jesus to take the wheel, right?

Then, from the corner of my eye, I noticed what appeared to be a yellow doorknocker advertisement lying on the ground. It was printed on a heavy card stock that has a prepunched hole for the doorknob with the advertising on both sides.

Most normal humans would have probably ignored it, but since I've been in real estate for a long time, I actually collect these kinds of things and study them to see what my competition is up to. I found it odd that a real estate agent would be canvassing property out in the boon-docks, so I put it in my pocket and continued on without even reading it.

Instead, I opened my car door, jumped in, and started up the car.

We left the house behind in a cloud of dust.

-3-

Take the Long Way Home

We rode in silence for several miles. After a while, Pastor Jim looked over at me.

"I know what you're thinking," he said. "You think that she's a hypocrite. She says one thing but does another. That is what you are thinking, isn't it?"

"Yeah, I guess so."

"Bob, you must love her, even if she annoys you."

I almost wanted to burst out in laughter but I knew he was being sincere.

"Let me finish my thought. You don't realize this Bob, but you are a true messenger of God."

I was dumbfounded. "Me?"

"Yes, you, Bob. Even though you think your efforts are about not getting sued, you are really helping Kelly and going beyond what a normal person might do. Fearlessly too, I might add."

I cracked a smile and thought, 'Please, don't make me laugh.'

"To be honest," I said, "I just want them to leave, I really do, without destroying the place, that's all I want."

"Well, God appreciates your efforts. That is why her husband is now in prison."

"I don't know about that one," I doubted.

"Bob, there are no coincidences in life. Last night, for example, her husband attacked a man that he thought was you and not only did he get beaten to a pulp, but he was brought to jail. That's pretty amazing, isn't it?"

I shrugged and nodded my head. "I guess so."

"Bob, just think if he was home today when we happened to knock on her door. Something terrible might have happened. So realize that you are blessed. God wants you to continue to be hopeful, and gentle, and kind, and patient just like you are doing. You are blessed."

"If you say so," I said. I actually told him that to make him feel better.

Pastor Jim looked at me. "I don't know if you know this,

but Kelly has lots of money. Why doesn't she just pay these people to leave?" he asked.

"She's tight with her money," I told him. "Kelly owned that house free and clear, and yet she refused to pay for fire insurance. That was another reason that I needed to close escrow fast on it, so the new buyer's fire insurance policy would kick in – just in case the tenants burned it down."

"Let me tell you something Bob," confided Pastor Jim. "When Kelly turned 35, her father left her over three million dollars."

"Yes, well, apparently the Curstons know this because after not paying rent for several months, their attorney wanted Kelly to pay $25,000 to get them to leave and she refused."

"Wait. They haven't paid rent in almost a year and he wants Kelly to pay them $25,000?"

"Exactly," I said. "So Kelly refused to pay a penny."

"Kelly has been taken advantage of by many people. Sometimes, she is not quite all there." He pointed to his temple. "She is a beautiful woman and physically she appears to be fine, but, but mentally she's... how would you call it? She's one taco short of a combo."

I grinned at his taco analogy.

When I finally dropped Pastor Jim off at his one-story bungalow, it was dark outside but he insisted that I come inside.

"I have something to give you," he insisted. "Please, Bob, it will only take a minute."

Considering he had wasted most of his day, I complied.

I followed him as he made his way inside the living room to a back office that was conspicuously religious. It was an average-sized room with a big L-shaped desk but the walls had stuff a religious fanatic would love. There were pictures of Jesus, crosses and shelves filled with books and holy things. The place smelled faintly of pipe tobacco and I was wondering if he was going to give me a gift. Perhaps a *Jesus Take the Wheel* cd? Instead, Pastor Jim held a large black book in one hand, and stood beside me with the other hand on my shoulder.

"Please, put your hand on this book Bob, and say these words after me," he instructed, so I put my hand as he had requested while he closed his eyes.

"Father, we pray that your love be with Bob and that you fill his heart with joy and that no harm be with him as he acts as a messenger for thee in thy holy service, and that all his burdens be lifted, and we ask this in the name of Jesus Christ, amen."

"Um, amen," I coughed. He had said everything too quickly

for me to repeat.

I was actually wondering if he was going to make me do it again when he turned his head. "There, did you hear that?" he asked me.

He reminded me of a dog that had been asked a calculus question.

"Hear what?" I said.

He nodded, like he had just heard something from a far-away distance.

"Your prayer will be answered Bob. You just have to believe it. All of this will fall behind you and no harm shall befall you."

Pastor Jim smiled at me as if he had outflanked the enemy somehow and I didn't really know what to believe. But I had to give him props for his positive thinking. Woo-hoo!

"Well, thank you for coming out to the house with me today," I said, "even though the trip there was a total bust."

"No, it wasn't a total bust, Bob, not at all. You'll see."

I stared up at him searching for a clue as to what I should do now.

He gave me a hug and I guess, for a moment or two, I wanted to believe him. But as I left his cottage and began to stride back to my car, I reached into my pockets for my car keys and pulled out the advertising paper that I had found at the property.

Once inside my car, I sat behind the wheel and switched on the inside light. I took a quick glance at the door hanger and almost had a heart-attack. It was not another piece of real estate advertising at all.

To my horror, I discovered the "doorhanger" was an official notice from the Los Angeles County Fire Department. It stated that the property owner had two weeks to clean up all the weeds and debris or he/she would be fined a whopping $11,000.

Kelly was no longer the owner. This meant that Mr. Juan Ortega would be fined $11,000 unless the weeds could be cut.

Shit. Would the Curstons even allow the weeds to be cut? I wondered.

What would happen if they didn't? With that, I made my way home.

-4-

LARRY AND THE
VACANT CONDO

My real estate office is located in a one-story building built in the late 1950s. With its flat roof it sort of resembles a big shoe box. Along with my office, there is a beauty salon next door and next door to that is a beer bar called Docs Inn.

The inside of my office spans about 1,400 sq. ft. and has three desks on one side of the room and three desks on the other. There is a receptionist's desk up front and a large conference room in the back.

That's where I was hiding, drinking a cup of coffee in the conference room.

The life of a real estate broker can change from bad to worse in 60 seconds. At nine o'clock, for example, you might receive a phone call from a buyer who says that he has "bad vibes" about the house he is purchasing and wants to cancel escrow. Then one minute after that happens, you might find that one of your agents has lost a listing that she has been working on for several months to a competitor. And then a minute after that you might even get a personal visit from an angry real estate agent about an agent in your firm.

At least that's what happened to me. On this particular day, a few months after my trip with Pastor Jim, I won the trifecta of bad news.

In my particular case, Tamera Moore, a gorgeous, young, shit-together blonde who represents the new breed of real estate agents, was the "angry" real estate agent paying me a visit.

Tamera looked to be about 27 but could probably pass for 18. Not only that, she had the reputation of being a smart, single woman who had thousands of followers on Twitter and Facebook. In other words: one wrong move on my part and my reputation would be toasted like a marshmallow over the bonfire of social media. Right now things did not look too rosy because Tamera was wearing an unhappy expression on her pretty face.

Crap. Just what I don't need. More drama.

Sylvia, our receptionist, brought Tamera straight to the conference room, unannounced so I could not ditch her by running out the back door like I had done to Sylvia in the past.

"Bob," she said," Tamera Moore would like to see you right now. That's okay, isn't it?"

Sylvia smirked as if to say, 'Gotcha. You can't run out this time.'

I got up and said, "Yes of course, that's perfectly fine. Have a seat, please, Miss Moore."

I pulled out a chair for the pretty blonde and Sylvia efficiently shut the door to give us privacy.

"First, please call me Tamera," she said. "Like camera."

"Okay, Tamera like camera. It's nice to meet you. Would you like some water or coffee?"

"No, thank you," she said. "I just wanted to reach out to you because I know you have worked in this valley for many years and people have told me that you are a nice guy and that I should speak to you in person first. So I wanted to do that before I went any further."

"Thank you. I can respect that." I added. "Um, what else do people say?"

"Good things, really. You're a lot younger-looking in person than your photograph."

"Well, thank you, and even though flattery will get you everywhere, I know you're upset and that's what is important.

So please tell me what's up? What brings you here?"

"Yesterday, I brought my client to one of your listings. A condominium in the Santa Fe development?"

"Ah, yes, the condo on Del Monte Drive," I said.

"Yes. Anyway, we saw the key in the doorknob so we knew that an agent had to be inside showing it, so I called out, 'Broker, broker,' but nobody answered."

"That's strange. Then what happened?" I prodded.

"Well there was a couch in the living room that blocked our view, but when we got closer, we could see that there was a man wearing a suit lying on the carpet. Flat on his back, arms stretched out. My buyer and I both thought he was dead."

"Really?!"

"Yes... So I kneeled down to touch his wrist to see if he had a pulse. Then suddenly, his eyes opened and he jumped to his feet!"

"My goodness!"

"Yes. My client and I both screamed! That's when he told us to calm down. He said his name was Larry and that he was a realtor in your firm. But the way he reached into his suit pocket, it seemed like he had a gun. We didn't want to end up murdered, so my client and I tore out of that place as fast as we could!"

"My god, I am so sorry this happened to you. You must have been scared to death!"

"I've never been so frightened in all my life. Anyway, when we got back to my office and explained it; one of my co-workers told me that this gentleman, Larry, does work for you. Is that true?"

I looked at her wanting to somehow deny it. But gazing in the window behind her, making rubbery faces like Jim Carey wearing a bad-fitting mullet toupee, was Larry Watkins, the very person she had been describing!

Lie, lie, lie, screamed my inner bad angel. But I couldn't. I nodded my head.

"Yes, he or she is right."

"I mean, this behavior is so... so unprofessional," she said as if not comprehending.

"Yes. I totally agree with you and I will see that he is severely punished."

She seemed sincere. "I was going to write something on my Twitter feed but everyone said to talk to you first. What do you think I should do?"

"Larry works part-time in real estate," I explained. "He's a single dad with two kids and works as a letter carrier during the day. So as much as I dislike what he did, I would rather have him sleeping somewhere, than driving around in a car and possibly injuring someone else. Do you know what I mean?"

"Yes, but still, it doesn't excuse his behavior."

"I totally agree. So I will be meeting with him today and I do appreciate you coming here and telling me personally and not sending out a Tweet or filing some kind of grievance with the board office."

"Well that still might happen. My broker is still talking about doing that."

"Okay, fair enough. I will leave that up to you, and if your broker Richard wants to talk with me about it, I would be more than happy to speak with him."

She rose from her chair. "Thank you so much for meeting with me," she said. "Hopefully we can do business soon."

She reached out and gave me a firm handshake.

"Looking forward to it," I said.

She shimmered away like a treasured object.

After she left, I breathed a sigh of relief as a much subdued Larry entered my office.

"Holy shit! Did you see the body on that chick? Man, I'd love to bang her like a screen door in a hurricane," he uttered loudly.

"Larry, she found you sleeping on the floor of a condo! What the hell were you thinking?" I chided him. "Taking a nap in a vacant condo?"

"Naps are for old people," he corrected. "I swear to you. I was taking a horizontal life pause."

"Gimme a break, Larry. A horizontal life pause?"

"Dude, I swear to you, I didn't mean to fall asleep. It's just that the carpet was so plush, and I was just so tired. I couldn't help it. I swear."

"This can't happen again, Larry, do you hear me? It's not funny."

"You're right. She coulda had a sharpie and drawn a huge dick on my face. That actually happened to me once at a frat party when I was in college."

"I bet," I said.

"No, it's actually true."

"And what was this about you pulling a gun on them?"

"Dude, it's not like I woke up with a massive boner or something. I was just reaching for a business card but my hand got caught on my inner pocket. I swear!"

I shook my head. Larry was a loser. But a lovable loser.

"Hey, did you see the ass on that chick? She's a hottie! Did she say anything about me?"

"Um, I think she said you reminded her of a guy she met on the highway the other night."

"Really?"

"Yeah. He was hitchhiking while wearing a hockey mask," I lied. "She thought he needed to go to hockey practice or something so she picked him up and gave him a ride."

I let the absurdity of that comment seep in, but it failed to do so.

"Wow," he exclaimed in utter fascination. My comment had apparently bent his mind. "A little creepy but that is sooo cool!"

There was a quick knock on the conference room door and then it opened. Sylvia, our stylish, late 40's receptionist was standing there. Sylvia volunteered at an animal shelter and was always concerned that our clients received immediate attention.

"Bob, there is a gentleman here to see you," she said.

I followed her to the front desk where a tall man wearing

a baseball cap was standing.

"Mr. Boog?" he said.

"Yes, that's me."

He handed me a large Manila envelope that resembled Priority Mail so I took it from him.

"What's this?"

"You've just been served. Have a nice day."

My heart sank as I opened the envelope and gazed at the paperwork. After all I had done for her, Kelly Mere was suing me.

-5-

SOME JUNE GLOOM ADVICE

My attorney Gerry's office is located at a two-story strip mall down the street from my office. There is a Carl's Jr. nearby and the other stores consisted of a massage parlor, a beauty salon and a nail salon. Asians rent almost every shop in the strip except for the law office.

When I entered my attorney's office, a little buzzer chimed and I heard him call out my name.

"Robert!" Besides my parents and former teachers, Gerald Steinman is the only person I know that calls me by my legal name. He is a short, unkempt, suit-wearing New Yorker with a thick head of silvery hair. There is a menorah on a bookshelf behind him with an autographed baseball encased in glass, but Gerry does not get up and simply waves his hand for me to take a seat.

"Tell me some good news, Robert. Tell me you've finally come to your senses and have filed a claim with your E&O

carrier." (Note: like most real estate brokers, I carry Errors and Omissions insurance ("E&O") to protect myself in case of damages and expenses as a result of a legal claim filed against me.)

"Um, not exactly," I said eyeing him.

"We talked about your case on the phone last night, right?"

"Gerry, I was just wondering if you have time for a drink. I'll buy. You like margaritas, don't you?"

"Sorry but I can't leave the office. I've got a 7:00 tonight. It's about the lady with the pony, right?"

"Why do you think it's about her?"

"I know you Robert," Gerry chuckled. "You wouldn't be offering to buy me a drink if you didn't want to pick my brain about something. You said she is suing you, right?"

"Well, not exactly. We're supposed to be going to arbitration in July so her lawyer gave me a list of arbitration companies." I showed Gerry the paperwork that I had most recently received. He glanced at it for a second. "Okay, it's exactly what I told you last night." he exclaimed. "You're fucked. She wants $24,000 that she lost because of the pony deal, plus another $17,000 for the damages due to the tenants ruining her property. It says so right here."

"Yeah, but I just realized, it's an arbitration hearing, not a lawsuit," I said.

He tossed it back on the desk.

"Robert, Robert, Robert. Get this through your head. She hired a big-name lawyer and this guy doesn't mess around. What Michael Phelps is to swimming and winning gold medals, Andy James is to business litigation. He never loses. He is going to chew you up and spit you out. You don't stand a chance against him."

For those of you unfamiliar with California real estate, to avoid expensive lawsuits, most real estate contracts include an "arbitration clause" that is initialed by both buyer and seller or in my case, seller and real estate agent. This clause states that any dispute will be handled by an independent arbitrator (usually an attorney or retired judge) and not a jury. However, either party is entitled to be represented by legal counsel at the arbitration hearing. What this means to you is that both Kelly and I could have an attorney represent us, and of course the attorney's fees for the winning party would be paid by the losing party.

"The thing is," I explained. "All of these arbitrators want a small fortune too."

"That, my friend, is why you should immediately file a claim. How much is the deductible on your E&O insurance?"

"Five grand," I answered.

"Okay. And how much will the arbitrator cost?"

"Another four grand."

"But that will be split between both parties 50/50 so a total of seven grand. Robert, that's cheap! Real estate litigation gets expensive. Very expensive! Especially if you lose the case! Robert, you don't have time to fool around with this. Your hearing comes up soon Robert; just pay the seven thousand and be done with it."

"Gerry, the problem is: I don't have seven grand. It's not like I have a tree that I can pull thousand dollar bills from."

Gerry pretended to play an imaginary violin. "Borrow it. You sell houses that cost close to half a million bucks. You make what, $14,000 every time you sell one?"

"C'mon Gerry," I whined. "I'm self-employed, the economy sucks. My wife's 85-year-old mother with dementia lives with us. I've got two kids in college who bleed me dry each month. Plus, I've got to pay for details such as gasoline, a mortgage and food. I can't borrow it from anybody. Right now my credit sucks."

"You can cry all you want Robert, but it's not going to change things," he chided me. "That's the chance you take with owning your own business. What do you want me to tell you?"

"I want you to tell me how we can get this lady to drop this lawsuit, that's what I want."

"We?" He repeated. "We?"

I looked at him.

"You haven't hired me, and I don't work for free," he said. "Let me tell you something, Robert. This lady, Kelly, is not going to drop this case. You know why? Because you failed her. You blew it. You were supposed to make up that paperwork for her pony prior to closing escrow, and you didn't do so, right?"

"Right, I didn't do it," I agreed.

"Therefore, she is going to take you for every penny she can because now that escrow has closed the buyer is not paying her, right?"

"Gerry," I whined, "I doubled her money in the worst real estate market since the great depression, plus, I found a notice from the fire department and was able to get gardeners into the place to cut down the weeds. That saved her from getting sued by the buyer. Plus I managed to evict her deadbeat tenants without them destroying or burning down her house– when she didn't have fire insurance. I did all this and she does this to me?"

"You want a medal?" my attorney glared at me. "Then join the army, but you're not gonna get one from me, or her."

"I can't believe it," I said.

"Well, figure a way to scrape together the money and hire an attorney. I mean, I would help you if I could, but I'm swamped."

"Here's the thing," I complained. "I didn't do anything wrong."

"Well, that's for the arbitrator to decide. What is admirable is how you managed to get those damn tenants out of that house. That's what I want to know. You should write a book about that. People would probably pay you good money for it. *Call it, How to Evict Your Nightmare Tenants* by Bob Boog. Seriously, how did you do it? How did you get them to leave?"

The truth is that both the Curstons and their attorney could not believe that I had closed escrow on Kelly's house without them knowing about it. So when Mrs. Curston had called me to complain about the rodent infestation in the house, I expressed genuine shock.

Rodent infestation. Remember how Kelly had rehabbed the entire house and made it look like a brand new home when the Curstons took possession?

So when Mrs. Curston told me that the house had become

infested with rodents and had called the Los Angeles County Health Department to complain, I did NOT get angry. Instead, I told her that she had done the right thing, and that if she could please fax me any information about it, I would greatly appreciate it. Then I reminded her, "Oh, by the way Mrs. Curston, Kelly is no longer the owner of the property."

"What?" Now it was her turn to express shock.

"Yes, we closed escrow a week ago. And because you do not have a rental contract with the new owner, she will be able to get you out quickly and easily. Have a nice day."

Click! I hung up the phone.

About ten minutes later, I received a panicked phone call from the Curstons' attorney. He demanded to know the name of the new owner. It was too early for the new owner's name to show up on the county ownership records, so I faxed him the HUD-1 closing statement to prove that Kelly no longer owned the house.

Then I simply asked him how much money it would cost to get the Curstons' to vacate the premises. "Give me a realistic number," I said. "Or the new owner would legally and quickly force them out."

And that is how I got the Curstons to finally walk away from the property and not destroy the house. I paid them off.

Of course the Curstons' attorney started out with $25,000 but as time dragged on and we got closer and closer to a court date for the unlawful detainer hearing, the number finally dropped down to $1,500. So I paid it. I didn't want the tenants to file for bankruptcy at the last minute in order to prolong things further.

The intervening months however, were not fun, and two important things happened. The first is that I convinced Kelly to hire a gardener to cut down the five acres of shoulder-high weeds. I told her that it was a fire hazard for the entire neighborhood, which it was.

And, because the tenants had filed a restraining order, Kelly could not enter the property, so I did, accompanied by two sheriff's deputies. I stayed and watched for a good 95 minutes while a gardener riding a lawnmower mowed the weeds.

During this time, of course, the entire Curston family picketed me with bad Christian rock music and their dutiful chants of, "It must suck to be Bob Boog."

Coincidentally, the new buyer happened to visit the property and witnessed me getting verbally abused by the tenants. He found it very strange.

"I do not think they like you," said the buyer, Juan Ortega, in what had to be the understatement of the year.

The second and equally important thing that happened occurred a while later, when accompanied by two sheriff deputies, Kelly visited the property and rescued her pony. She had feared that the Curstons had not been feeding or giving it water, so, she brought a horse trailer to the property and absconded with it.

* * *

Back to reality: me sitting with my attorney. Gerry shook his head.

"Well, all I can say is this Robert: you were supposed to have the buyer sign a note and deed of trust for $24,000 prior to closing escrow and you didn't do so. Believe me, getting this woman Kelly to drop the case against you, is not going to happen. She is going to want her pound of flesh."

I left Gerry's office feeling hopeless and like my innocence was caught between the crossfire of Kelly's anger and arbitration fees.

I needed some retail therapy, so I visited the Vons grocery store and purchased four bottles of Cabernet wine and two bottles of Zinfandel.

The attractive-looking cashier who rang up the purchase

seemed a bit surprised. "Looks like somebody's going to be having a good time tonight," she commented.

"Yeah, you're right. I sure did buy a lot of alcohol," I worried. "Hope I'm not turning into a shopaholic."

She gave me a look. "Will this be everything?" She flashed a pretty smile.

"Um, no. I'd like to buy all this invisible shit too," I said pointing at the empty black conveyor belt.

She grinned, shook her head and gave me a sideways eye that said, "Smart ass".

-6-

MY NEW NIGHTMARE

A few days after meeting with my attorney, I got a phone call from Mr. Juan Ortega, the buyer of Kelly's house. So now, not only did I have a problem with Kelly suing me for $24,000 plus damages for the pony and $17,000 plus damages for the house, but now Juan was calling me too.

"Hi, Mr. Bob. This is Juan Ortega, and you probably don't remember me but I bought the house here in Agua Dulce. The one with the pony?"

How could I ever forget, I thought to myself. Now what?

"Oh, yes, I think I remember," I said calmly. "How can I help you?"

"Well, it rained this last weekend, and a big inundation of water came down the mountain and into my living room. It was never disclosed to me that a flood like this could happen. Can you come over here and look at the damage to my property caused by this flooding?"

"Certainly, I can, but Mr. Ortega, let me remind you I was

not your agent. I was representing the seller, remember? What happened to your agent?"

"I am sorry, Mr. Bob but my agent quit real estate. You see, all of the stress from buying this house and evicting the tenants caused him to have a very serious ulcer. The doctors had to cut two feet of his intestines out you know, and they told him never to work again in real estate."

Just my luck. That little delusion that somebody else might help me out danced right out of my head.

"Okay, I will stop by and check out the damage."

"Thank you so much. I really appreciate it."

For those of you unfamiliar with California weather it rarely rains, but when it does, just a tiny sprinkle can cause major freeway accidents, mudslides, and flash flooding.

I drove out to the property to assess the damage. What a depressing sight. Six-to-eight inches of mud had flash-flooded throughout the house, and, as he said, there was a lot of damage – including a big-screen TV that had fallen. Apparently the place had also flooded during the time when the Curstons lived there, too, because Juan pointed out mold growing in bluegreen patches from the bottom of the living room drywall.

I dimly recalled when Kelly had purchased the property

from the bank, a shed and a cinder block wall had protected the back of the house. Obviously, looking back, it had been placed strategically in the path of where this river of water would go. But when Kelly had renovated the property, she had removed both so now there was nothing to divert water that rushed down the mountain to the house.

Next, Mr. Ortega took me into the kitchen and pointed to the ceiling. I could see a big hole where daylight showed through. A bucket had been placed on the floor to collect the water and so it was obvious that the roof leaked. Kelly had signed a counter offer where she had agreed:

To sell the pony to the buyer for $24,000 secured by a note with monthly payments of $345 per month.

She had also agreed to pay to remove the tenant and pay for the buyer's house payment while the eviction was taking place.

Fix the roof to make it watertight. (The buyer had paid for a home inspection and the home inspector had noted a hole in the roof in his report.)

Now, to this day, people ask, "How were the buyers able to get a home inspection, appraisal and termite report done on the property, if the tenants were so uncooperative?"

Because, for those of you who are not familiar with buying a home, usually these inspections happen days or weeks apart. The normal procedure goes as follows:

Day 1: the buyer and seller agree on a price and open escrow.

Days 2-15: the buyer pays for a home inspector to check out the condition of the property. The inspector gives an extensive report which often includes walking on the roof, going up in the attic, checking every electrical outlet, crawling under the house, etc.

Days:15-25: the purchaser then pays for an appraisal of the house. This individual photographs the interior and exterior of the house, as well as takes pictures of comparable properties in the area that have recently sold or are listed.

Days: 1-30: the seller will hire a pest control inspector to ensure that there is no wood damage or pests such as termites that might damage the property in the future.

Most inspections are spread out over the course of the entire escrow period which takes from 30 – 60 days.

Please note: on the phone Ms. Curston sounded extremely accommodating, but I didn't trust her completely either. Therefore, I decided to have all the contractors arrive at the house on the same day.

I needed the tenants to be there as well, because they

were the only ones who had access to the property as Kelly claimed she could not find her keys.

However, on the day of the inspection, NONE of the tenants were home. When I called Ms. Curston's cell phone, she told me they had gone to San Diego and would not be home for a few days. Great.

So try to imagine the scene: there I am, along with a tribe of people standing around the front door of the house, while I knock and knock and knock. A tall appraiser wearing a baseball cap was busy measuring the exterior of the property, a home inspector wearing overalls had pushed his ladder to the side of the house and had begun climbing onto the roof to examine its condition. The termite guy was there and of course there was the selling agent Jorge, wearing a suit and tie and shiny shoes. The buyers, Juan and Maria Ortega were there, along with their beautiful, long-haired ten year old daughter. Like many people of modest means, the Ortegas were decked-out in their Sunday best, with Mrs. Ortega holding her daughter's hand in a firm, death-like grip.

My apologies for being stupid and believing these yahoo's would be here, I thought to myself as I knocked and knocked. Nothing. Then I used my cell phone and listened to the Curstons' message telling me they had decided to visit San Diego. Inside, I was thinking. They are laughing their asses off because they are making me look like an idiot!

"Is anybody home?" somebody asked.

"No, it doesn't look like it." I said.

I turned around to face the firing squad.

"Mr. Bob, what is going on?" Juan Ortega demanded. He spoke in a thick accent. Juan was a slender, average-looking man with an uncommon amount of patience. His face lifted up to me and I could see the wrinkles near his mouth and large brown eyes, and I knew that it had probably taken years of hard work and self-sacrifice to save for his down payment. I truly respect people like Juan Ortega and wanted to help him buy this home.

At this point, Jorge, the selling agent with the shiny shoes began to whine. "I can't believe that we all took one hour of our valuable time to drive all the way out here. This is so un-professional." Blah, blah, blah, blah, blah.

Luckily, I list homes for banks. And most banks are so cheap they will often re-key homes using the same master key for all of them. And since Kelly had originally purchased the home from a bank, I decided to try one of the bank keys that was on my key ring, and guess what happened? BAZIN-GA! One of the random keys on my keychain unlocked the front door. Woo-hoo!

Jorge had to stop complaining in mid-bitch because I gingerly swung open the door. "Hello! Broker," I called out.

I paused before entering because sometimes a house seems empty, but suddenly, a big dog will leap out and gag itself at the end of its chain and scare the shit out of you.

Empty. Not a peep came from inside. Jackpot!

Thus, unknown to the tenants, all of the inspections, disclosures and appraisals were done while the Curstons were in San Diego! For this reason, the tenants never had a clue about the pending sale of the house.

* * *

Getting back to Juan's house, I took some photographs using my cell phone and decided to ask him a couple of questions.

"Do you remember that you had agreed to pay $345 per month for the pony?"

"Oh yes, Mr. Bob, I do. Every month we put away the exact amount for the pony, even though we never received any papers from the seller."

"That's good."

"Yes, Mr. Bob. That is what our attorney advised us to do."

Oh, great. Another attorney, I thought. This just keeps getting better.

"Mr. Bob I do not know if I should tell you this, but my attorney is ready to sue you and the seller. We have told her 'No, that you are a good man.'"

"Thank you, Juan, I appreciate that."

"But of course, if you cannot figure out a way to help me to fix this damage here, I do not know what we are going to do. If we must pursue our legal remedies, to resolve our situation, then of course, yes we will."

"Yes, I understand."

"We trust you will do something, Mr. Bob."

"I will do my best," I promised.

After pumping his hand, I made it back to car and cruised back to my office. A thousand thoughts sizzled like bacon in my head, but I wasn't sure of what I should do next.

I decided the only way the meeting with Juan could have been more disappointing was if it had been an M. Night Shyamalan film.

-7-

MIKE MITCHELL

A small plaque on the front door of the two-story house I was standing in front of read "NO SOLICITORS." In real estate, even though you may be having a bad day in one part of your business, you must continue to prospect for more buyers and sellers and that's exactly what the new agent Mike Mitchell and I were doing. We were trying to drum up business by knocking on doors and asking homeowners if they wanted to sell.

A tall, lanky 33 year old, Mike Mitchell resembles Will Farrell and stands about 6'3", but with his thick head of curly hair he looks taller.

"Why would you knock on this door?" he complained. "The sign clearly says, 'No Solicitors'. And we are soliciting, aren't we?"

"I didn't even see a sign," I lied, knocking again on the door. "Look, people tell me that I'm out of touch all the time."

"You're out of touch?" Mike said checking my eyes.

"Yeah, the other day my wife told me I was out of touch and I almost peed my Hammer pants."

"Funny. See, you can say shit like that because you're married," he complained. "I can't because I'm single. Being single sucks."

"Okay, now what are you going to say if somebody answers the door?" I asked, changing the subject before Mike turned morose. Mike sometimes looked at the half-empty side of the wine bottle.

"Dude, nobody is gonna answer. We've been out schlepping around for over an hour and only three people have even answered, and all three just slammed the doors in our faces."

Mike had a point. So far we had visited over 165 homes and had managed to meet only a small handful of occupants. This home seemed different though. I had a good feeling about it. Truth is, I could hear the sound of children's laughter coming from inside.

"Think positive. Now, what are you gonna say?" I repeated.

"My name is Mike, and I'm a broker in your area, and I was wondering if you wanted to sell your home."

"Wrong," I corrected. "Nobody wants to sell anything. But ask them if they've ever thought about making a move? That's different. Lots of people like to think about moving."

"Why do I have to say I'm a broker when I'm not? You're the broker, not me."

"Broker is just a fancy term for real estate agent. When you call a real estate office, for example, do you say, 'Real estate agent call' or 'Broker call?'"

"Broker call," he answered.

"Right. And when you enter a house and you're not sure whether someone is home, do you yell out, 'Real Estate Agent' or 'Broker?'"

"Broker," he answered.

"See, there you go."

The door suddenly swung open, revealing a buxom blonde wearing a black bikini with dark sunglasses. She looked like she jumped straight out of the Playboy channel. Her caramel-mocha-latte skin accented her deep cleavage, and she wore her long, straight blonde hair in a ponytail. In her mid 30's, the gorgeous woman held a red plastic cup and smelled a bit like alcohol and suntan lotion.

"Can I help you?" she asked in a sultry, accent sounding Swedish.

"Hi, my name is Mike and I'm and I'm," Mike stuttered, "I mean, you wanna move?"

She paused before she lifted her sunglasses. "Yes, actually I might like to move. I am Hilda." The two shook hands.

"Really!" Mike sputtered incredulously and turned to me for help. "Now what?" He looked at me as if Hilda didn't exist.

"Something happen?" I blathered.

"Yes, my husband and I split up, so, I'm going to have to do something. Would you like to come inside?"

Mike looked at me.

"Of course we would," I responded.

The two of us followed in Hilda's wake as she entered the house. The place looked like it had been the victim of a search warrant and the police had rummaged through everything. There were piles of toys, dirty dishes and clothes everywhere on the floor. A television was on, and coincidentally the talking head onscreen belonged to none other than attorney Andy James offering to help victims of "real estate fraud" cases. "Hablamos español" a deep voice thundered at the end of the commercial.

"It looks like you were in the middle of cleaning," I lied. "We could come back later."

"No, it's fine."

She turned off the TV. "This is the living room," she pointed.

"My ex-husband made the mantel on the fireplace."

"Very nice," Mike gushed.

"I hate it," she said quickly.

We followed Ms. beautiful, sexy, hot girl into the hot mess of her kitchen. Dishes were stacked up and leaning in the sink like a *Cat in the Hat* book. Any minute now, the plates could crash. She had obviously been drinking heavily because she tossed her plastic red cup in the trash and put the half-empty Gallo jug back into the fridge.

"Where are your kids?" I asked.

"Their dad has them this weekend," she said. She gave Mike the once-over before asking, "Are you married?"

"Nope, single."

"Straight or gay?"

"Straight." Mike made a nervous gesture knocking a potted ficus off a stack of magazines. That was one thing I noticed about Mike: how nervous he got when he was one-on-one with women. Lance Romance does it again.

She picked up the broken pieces of the pot and set them on the kitchen counter. "Don't worry about it. I was planning on tossing it anyway."

She was barefoot and we both could see her butt crack as

she bent down again to pick up the broken pieces of the pot and throw them away. Lordy, lordy, lordy.

Mike's eyes bulged like a teenager viewing his first Playboy centerfold.

"Let me show you the rest of the house."

She padded down the hallway to the closed rooms. Two of the doors she opened, which allowed us to vaguely see inside, but the third door, she didn't open. "I'm renting this room," she explained. "And this is my bedroom."

She pulled the last door open to reveal a darkened room reminding me of going into a seedy porn theater but instead of a movie screen there was a large four-poster bed, night tables, and a dresser. It smelled like roses. Some sexy, frilly underwear hung from a red lampshade. If these walls could talk.

Before we departed, she wrote her phone number on a post-it note and gave it to Mike. "Call me, okay? I really want to know how much this place is worth."

She fussed with her hair while looking into a little make-up mirror.

Mike nodded. "I'll do my breast." Pause "Um, best" he corrected.

"How soon would you like us to return?" I asked.

"Tonight, around 7:30?" she told Mike.

Mike nodded his head quickly, glancing over at me as if asking for approval.

"She wants YOU to come over, dude, not me," I gently chided.

"Why sure. Um, yes, yes, of course yes. I'll be here tonight at 7:30."

We made it out of the house and continued on for a little while before Mike busted out a loud "Woo-hoo! Did you SEE that chick? I mean, I've seen women like that in *Penthouse*, but never, ever, ever in real life!"

I could tell Mike had love-making in his head. It was as plain as the day when the weather-lady's nipples on TV firmed up under her silk blouse.

"Yeah, well, remember; don't just be like the pizza boy in the porn movie. Real estate is about making money too."

We continued on knocking on doors and Mike finally caught up to me to compare notes.

"Dude, you gotta admit she was frickin' hot!"

"Yes," I agreed, "she was hot."

Hopefully her ex-husband isn't a deranged psycho too, I thought.

-8-

LARRY'S MARKETING IDEA

Larry approached me at the conference room and told me he had a great idea for promoting our company. Since I am all ears about marketing and getting our name publicized, I told him to explain in detail what he had in mind.

"You probably don't know this about me," Larry started, "but I am a wonderful piano player. So I was thinking about playing piano at the fourth of July parade."

"That's it? I thought you had a marketing plan of some type," I questioned.

"It is a marketing scheme. I will put our Bob Boog Realty sign on the side of my player piano, and as we drive by, folks will watch me play the piano; and they will identify my playing with this company. What do you think?"

He gave me an impish-looking Jim Carrey-like grin.

It's better than finding you sleeping at a vacant house, I

thought.

"How many people are going to be at the parade?" I asked.

"Dude, at least six thousand. Possibly as high as ten thousand."

"Okay," I said. "Let's do it."

"There's just one thing," Larry stated, "I'll need your help loading the piano onto my trailer."

"How heavy is this piano?"

"It's pretty heavy," he admitted. "But I've done it before with two people."

"Okay, no problem, I'll help you," I said.

"What are you working on?" he asked.

"I'm just trying to get ready for my arbitration hearing. I'm supposed to go before the judge in two weeks."

"That's the lady with the pony, right?"

"Yep, I call it my nightmare."

"I don't get it," he said. "Why didn't you just do what you were supposed to do?"

His face still wore a grin.

"It's not like I forgot to do it or that I was negligent," I explained.

"Then what happened? Why didn't you do it?"

"Let me ask you a question, Larry. How would you identify a horse that you barely ever saw?"

"I don't know," Larry answered. "By its color?"

"Good try but the correct way to do it," I said, "is to fill out a Bill of Sale. So before the close of escrow, I called Kelly and asked her to bring me all the vet bills she had on the pony. I figured maybe there was an identification number on a vet bill I could use to identify the pony somehow because I had never really examined the pony."

"And what did she say?"

"Kelly refused to bring me the paperwork. In fact, she told me that she intended to switch the pony for another one that she was going to buy."

"That's fucked up," Larry said.

"I agree. Especially if the buyer has a bright-eyed ten year-old girl who used to feed the pony carrots every time they came up to the house. So I told the seller, 'No, you have to get someone else to make up the paperwork.' I asked her to call her eviction attorney to see if he could do it, so Kelly called me back and said, 'Yes, he could do it,' so I said, 'Great. Have him do it then' because I did NOT want to be a part of switching Kelly's pony. To me, that would be committing fraud."

"What did your attorney say when you told him that?"

"My attorney said I still should have done it. He claims, the seller could have left a better horse for the buyer, but to me, legal or not, this just didn't seem right. Besides, I still have to face myself in the mirror. What if she bought a lame horse or what if the animal had some kind of disease?"

Larry shook his head, "I think you did the right thing, but it's kind of ironic, isn't it? She can defraud the buyer, and yet, turn around and sue you for fraud."

"Exactly," I answered. "It doesn't seem fair."

"My dad used to do shit like that," Larry said. "He would buy patio furniture at Home Depot every spring and even leave the price tags on it. Then when fall would arrive, he would bring the furniture back claiming it was all defective – just so he could get his money back."

I have got to remember that trick, I thought to myself. That is genius.

"Who is Kelly's attorney?" Larry asked.

"A guy named Andy James."

"Andy James?" Larry repeated. "The guy on all the TV commercials?"

"Yeah, what do you know of him?"

Larry shook his head. "My ex-wife hired him. Biggest prick in town. Pompous asshole. Graduated from Harvard. Charges people five hundred bucks an hour. One more thing: that dude has never, ever lost a case!"

"Um, thanks for the vote of confidence," I said.

"You ARE still gonna help me though with the piano, right?"

"Yes, I will help you with your piano."

"Thanks, man."

-9-

KELLY'S VISIT

Dressed in jeans and riding boots, Kelly Mere stepped out of her white Toyota pickup truck and moved towards the glistening glass doors of the modern office building. Once entering the building she made her way to an elevator and pressed the button for the 4th floor.

Upon exiting, she moved down the hallway and stopped near the sign which read: James & Associates Law Firm.

An attractive looking receptionist smiled as Kelly entered. "Hi, may I help you?" she said.

"Hi, my name is Kelly Mere. I am here to see Mr. James."

"Have a seat, please." the receptionist purred. She then made a quick call, "Mr. James, a Kelly Mere is here to see you?"

Kelly sat down and waited for a few seconds until the receptionist responded with, "Mr. James will see you now. Follow me."

Kelly followed the receptionist to Mr. James' private office and entered.

"Kelly, it's good to see you again," said Andy James. He was a lean man with an eastern accent who was wearing a grey, tweed jacket and silver wire-rimmed glasses. "Welcome to my hillbilly hotel," he joked.

Kelly marveled at the bronze sculptor of a horse which was sitting on his desk.

"This is nice," she said. "Do you ride?"

"Nah, this is the closest I've ever been to a horse."

"Oh," she sounded a bit disappointed.

"So what brings you here today Miss Mere?"

"I just want to know what my chance is," Kelly said, sitting down.

"Your chance?"

"Of winning my case. Sorry, arbitration hearing."

"Your chance? Your chance is 100 per cent," he said confidently. "Your case is a slam dunk."

"You're sure, now."

"Yes. Why would you think anything different?"

Kelly gave him a nervous smile.

"Because you don't know him. Mr. Boog is a very smart

man."

Andy chuckled. "Your real estate agent is smart?"

She nodded.

"Well, smart-ass might be more accurate," he said. "But he screwed up, big time. I guarantee you."

"Well, I want him to pay for his mistake," she piped up. "I want him to hurt."

"This sounds personal."

"Have you ever loved a kitty-cat?" she asked. She continued before he could answer. "I own seven cats, and I love all of them. But my favorite cat was named Jamie. He was a calico and one morning, he went missing. I looked all over for him but couldn't find him. I figured the coyotes probably got him."

"Yes, that happens."

"And when Mister Boog came over, I told him what happened to my Jamie, and do you know what he told me?"

Andy shrugged. No idea.

"He asked me if I had looked inside my pickup truck."

"That's what he said?"

"Yes, then he said, 'Maybe your cat thought outside the litter box' or something "smart-alecky" like that. Can you believe that? Like I would purposely leave the window open for my baby kitty-cat to stay inside my truck. What a jerk!"

Andy squirmed in his chair, thinking to himself he was dealing with a monster cat lady, but outwardly, he nodded understandingly.

"To me, cats are like little women wearing fur coats," he offered.

"How so?" she asked.

"See, cats are like women because they do what they want, when they want. Cats are moody like women and rarely listen to you. Cats are unpredictable, like women. They whine when they're not happy. They leave their hair everywhere, but I love cats, just like I love women."

"I am so glad I met you!" Kelly gushed.

Andy rose from his chair and clasped her hand, "Don't you worry about a thing, Kelly. You will have your money in no time, and we will teach Mr. Boog a hell of a lesson. One he will never forget!"

-10-

MY WIFE'S SUGGESTIONS

During the days leading up to the arbitration hearing, my face began to look more somber and ruined by the lack of sleep. Most of the time I acted like the Great Oz who anonymously pulled the whistles and levers behind a happy real estate façade. Inside, I lived with a constant sick feeling in my stomach. I didn't have a good feeling about the way things were going. I felt doomed.

And every day, the moment of truth drew closer and closer.

Truth is, I am a doubter too. I generally got good grades in school because I over-studied. I have succeeded in real estate because I worry about things. I tend to be passive-aggressive about it. I'll pretend like everything is no big deal. If I smell smoke and see a cloud of in the distance, for example, I will immediately panic and assume that it's our house that's on fire. But outside I'll be like, "I'm not concerned about a fire, besides, it's probably someone else's house on my street." Inside I'm dying to drive to the house to see if I left the iron on again.

Recently, my doctor suggested that I needed to reduce stress. He suggested I take a yoga class. Great, I thought. Now I have that to worry about.

My wife, Roxana almost never worries. Roxy works as a licensed real estate agent with me. Roxy is an attractive, strong, yet feminine, Hispanic woman who was born and raised in Guatemala City. Two years younger, slender and much prettier than me, Roxy stands about 5'6 and has brown skin, almond-shaped eyes, and black hair. Roxy never attended college yet is one of the smartest people I know. After all, she married me, right?

Plus Roxy is blessed with the rare, uncommon gift of being "street smart."

What this means to you is that she possesses common sense and an uncanny intuition which enables her to easily cut to the chase of a problem or situation.

One morning, for example, I started to tell her about a dream I had and she interrupted me with: "If you honestly think I want to hear about the details of your dream, then you're still fucking dreaming."

That's what I mean. Roxy is very direct and doesn't mince words.

When it came to the pony situation and I laid it all on the line for her, she looked at me and said: "Don't you remember? You told me all this shit before."

I gave her a dumb look. "I did?"

"Yes, that's why I took Gerry's advice and called our Errors and Omissions Company."

"What did they say?" I asked.

"They won't touch it. Seems like the pony idea maybe wasn't such a keen idea after all."

"But that's why we pay them a monthly fee, to cover things like this," I complained.

"Well, apparently making a loan against a pony is outside the realm of their coverage," she said. "Look, the buyer claims that he was damaged due to the seller not disclosing the flooding issue, right? Can't you use that angle with the seller?"

"Possibly," I said. "But the buyer is making an implied threat against me. Like, if I can't make something happen for him, right away, the buyer wants to turn around and sue me."

"Well, figure that he probably will sue you, so find out if the seller did disclose it. And if the flooding issue was disclosed, show it to the buyer. But if she didn't disclose it, don't tell the buyer, at least not for a while."

"Okay, good idea," I said.

What this means, for those of you who are not involved in real estate, is this: if there is a material defect with a house before escrow closes, and an agent fails to disclose it, the agent can be sued. The seller can write, for example, "this home will fall down in two weeks because of a bad foundation." But as long as the buyer signs a written disclosure to that effect prior to closing escrow, the defect has been disclosed and the agent is safe. If not, the agent can be sued.

"When is your hearing?" she asked me.

"About a week from today."

"If I were you," she said, "I would call up her attorney and see if he can give you a little more time. You have nothing to lose and everything to gain."

With those two suggestions in mind, I decided to revisit the disclosures in the file. By state law, real estate agents are required to keep all files of offers made, rejected and cancelled, for three years. So there were a lot of files but this one was easy to locate.

In addition, because of the tenant eviction and notes made, there was quite a bit of paperwork to sift through. But lo and behold and much to my surprise, Kelly DID disclose she had a flooding issue. Woo-hoo! This disclosure had been signed by both buyer and seller too, so at least I had some protection if the buyer did try to sue me.

After that, I called Kelly's attorney on the phone but he didn't pick up so I left him a voice message that went:

"Hi Mr. James, this is Bob Boog and I'm reaching out to you because you gave me a list of arbitrators and I can't seem to locate an available one any time soon. Can you please call me back?"

We played telephone tag five or six times, but when I finally got to speak with him, Andy seemed like an alright guy.

"My schedule is a bit tight right now," he said in a nasally, thick, east-coast accent, "Let's make it for the middle of August," he told me. "My calendar will be a bit more open then."

Whew! I felt like I'd been given a last-minute reprieve from death row by the governor. I now had one additional month to find an arbitrator or lawyer or both.

Then I almost jumped out of my chair when my cell phone rang. It was Larry calling me. I picked up. "Dude, are you gonna make it or not?"

"Make what?" I asked.

"My piano, remember? You said that you were gonna help me today."

"Right, right. I'm leaving right now!" I said and ran to my car and started driving.

Larry lived in Pine Mountain Club, which lies about one hour north of my office. As the crow flies, it is situated about 60 miles east of Santa Barbara in the mountains. A winding two-lane road through tall pine trees brings one to a valley where there is a general store, a gas station and a two-story building with other small business shops.

The piano was housed in Larry's single-story manufactured home, located a few blocks from the general store. It was a vintage, oak, upright player-style piano he had purchased at an estate sale. Larry had lovingly taken apart the entire piano piece by piece, stained the wood, put it back together, and then had the piano professionally tuned. It was his baby.

He had rented a piano mover which is a four wheel dolly for moving heavy objects, and because the porch of his manufactured home was slightly higher than the trailer, we were able to use the gate of the trailer as a ramp. With the aid of the four-wheeled piano mover, the two of us were able to guide, push, and pull the piano onto the trailer without too much of a struggle. Bringing it back into the house, I mentally calculated, would probably require much more effort and maybe even more man-power.

Once the piano was safely inside the U-haul horse-trailer, Larry wrapped it lovingly in a few blankets and then secured the piano with rope and bungee cords.

He then had me double-check the brake lights of the trailer to see that they were working properly. They were, so I gave him a "thumbs up" and then I followed him in my car back to Santa Clarita, where I helped him unload the piano at a local elementary school. The entire trip took about three hours, so we made good time.

That night I went to bed early, exhausted by the drive and moving the heavy piano, and I was awoken by my cell phone ringing. It was 2:25 in the morning, and the person's name that showed up on my iPhone's register was KELLY.

I thought about answering the phone, but then decided against it, and fell back asleep.

-11-

KELLY'S MESSAGE

I listened to Kelly's voice message in disbelief.

Then I put her message on my iPhone's speakerphone so that my wife could hear it too. Kelly started out by slurring her words, and since getting drunk first is always a signature move if you want to avoid being the designated driver, I mentally commended her.

"Hello, Mr. Boog, this is Kelly Mere. I am very angry with you. You made me buy a pony for those effing Mexican people and I completed my part of the deal. I brought a new pony to those fucking Mexicans and I didn't have to. Where is my money? I want my $24,000! Why did you do this to me? I hate you! I effing hate you!" The message cut off with a click.

"Um, I don't think she likes you," my wife observed.

"Yeah, well, I don't think she likes the buyers either," I added. "Did you hear how she called them fucking Mexicans?"

"That lady should be grateful that even though she rented to those people against your advice, you were able to sell that property and close escrow," my wife said. "Most likely those redneck renters were going to sue her for getting hit by that metal pipe. It wasn't your fault the court system in Los Angeles takes such a long time to process an eviction."

"Yes, but in a strange way, this message helps me," I said. "Think about it. She just admitted to committing fraud."

"No, she didn't." my wife argued.

"She said, 'You made me buy that pony for those people'" I told her. "But the truth is, I never made her buy any pony. She was supposed to sell her existing pony to them, not buy a new one."

"The pony was just something to make a loan for $24,000," my wife argued. "It's not all that important. Like your attorney said, she can claim that she bought them a better pony. I just think you need something else."

"The question is, why did she call me?" I wondered.

* * *

I thought about the phone message all the way to the office and was still thinking about it before our weekly meeting in the office conference room.

As mentioned, the conference room is just a big private room located near the back of the office. There is a door that leads into the room that can be closed to help keep the rabble down, and inside is a long wooden table and some chairs that surround it.

My top-producing agents: Larry Watkins, Mike Mitchell, and Sandy Johnson were seated and waiting for me to join them for our weekly half-hour session. Roxy was busy and couldn't make it, and Sylvia was at the front desk putting labels on envelopes and manning the phones in case someone called.

I wanted to get the gang's feedback on the recording, but before I could start, I had to endure the inevitable back-and-forth chatter that happens before we get started each week.

On this day, Mike was giving Larry crap about being single. "I mean, it must suck being single and knowing that a guy as repulsive as Hitler was able to find a date but YOU can't find one."

Larry shrugged it off. "I'm just waiting for the right girl."

Mike replied: "You DO know that finding an attractive, millionaire blond who lives in Hawaii is a myth, right?"

"Not even my type," Larry returned. "I just want a normal girl. Nothing fancy. One who has a great sense of humor about being a supermodel," he said sarcastically.

"Yeah, right."

"Hey, loneliness can make girls do some strange people,"

Sandy said. "Not that I would ever consider stooping to doing someone as strange as you or anything."

Everyone looked at Sandy who was 45 pounds over-weight and engaged to a man who lived three hours away who everybody thought was married.

"Okay, listen to this and tell me what you think," I said.

Everyone listened as I replayed Kelly's message on speakerphone.

Sandy, being the only blonde in the bunch, came up with this observation: "Simple. She drunk dialed you. It's 2:30 in the morning. Kelly secretly likes you. Why else would a woman drunk dial someone?"

Mike smirked, "Here's a fun fact for you: most drunk dialers know the people they dial."

Larry looked at him. "I think it is annoying that some people think facts are fun. In any case, not sure if anyone else has any experience with drunk dialing," Larry continued, "but let's just say that maybe if you don't remember dialing, it didn't happen. Just throwing it out there. You've probably never done it. Have you?"

Ms. Johnson hitched her fleshy shoulder.

"Okay, yes, I'm guilty," she admitted. "I have drunk dialed my boyfriend."

"I prefer dirty talk while drunk dialing," Mike added.

"She's obviously a rookie. I mean, why leave a voice mail?" Larry wondered. "Because your friends can let their friends have fun at your expense for days, or even weeks to come."

"If you are going to drunk dial someone you know," said Mike, "like your mom, a close friend, or real estate agent, at least say something nice."

I looked at Mike. "Your mom? You drunk-dialed your mom?!"

He shrugged.

"Not on purpose," He explained. "Me and my friends were bored one night so we drank a bunch of beer and started drunk dialing people out of the phone book. This guy handed me the phone and said, 'Go for it' so I did. After I was finished telling the chick how I wanted to bend her over and bang her doggie style, I heard the familiar voice of my mother saying, "OMG, Michael, is that you?"

"Oh my god, how embarrassing!" Sandy cried.

"Needless to say, I wasn't very happy with my so-called friends."

"Let's get back to Kelly," I said, changing the subject. "Seriously, why do you think she called me?"

"Maybe she just got her bill from her attorney," Larry said sarcastically.

"What does that have to do with anything?" Sandy asked.

"Well, when I was going through my first divorce," Larry explained. "My first attorney charged me for the phone calls he received from other people."

"No way," Mike said. "He charged you for receiving phone calls?"

"Yep. He said they were involved in the case."

"They do charge you for every little thing," Sandy offered. "My brother-in-law was an attorney and he hated it because he was always under pressure to bill more hours."

That's when it dawned on me. Calling Kelly's lawyer more often might be something to consider. As world famous chess player Bobby Fischer once said, "In chess, your best defense is a strong offense."

Perhaps that should be my new strategy. Play harder on offense.

-12-

THE MAN FROM INDIA

One hour later, I was still contemplating the "go on the offense" strategy when a bearded man from India entered our office. He had on a white linen robe with sandals on his feet, and he wore a black turban.

I happened to be leaving the office, so I practically bumped into him.

"Excuse me sir, do you know where the train station is located?" he asked.

"Um, it's about five miles away," I said. "Why?"

"My train leaves at two o'clock."

I checked the clock on the wall. It showed ten minutes to two.

"You will never get there in time walking," I said. "Look, I can give you a ride."

"You would do that for me?"

"Certainly."

He was licking his lips, so I gave him the bottle of water I had just taken out of the fridge for myself and handed it to him. "Here, take this," I offered. "I think you need it more than me."

"Thank you. You are very kind."

He got in my car and gulped down the water as I drove.

"What's your name?" I asked.

"My name is Yogi."

"And I'm Boo-Boo," I joked. He apparently was not smarter than the average bear because he did not find any humor in my joke.

We drove in silence for a while.

"What brings you here to Santa Clarita?" I asked.

"I am a holy man."

"From India, right?"

"Yes. I am from India. But I have traveled all across the United States."

"Ahh, that's cool," I said. "How is the holy work going?"

The awkward pause when someone senses you are not at all being serious.

"You do not seem very religious."

"Not really." I said.

"Are you not a Christian?" he asked.

"No, not really," I said. "Are you?"

"No, but it just seems unusual, especially in this country."

"Christians focus mainly on his death and resurrection," I said. "I just don't believe it's all that important. But some of his stories are cool. There is one story for example when Jesus goes fishing with his friends. They can't catch a single fish so he tells them to throw their nets on the other side of the boat and, sure enough, they get lucky. That story has always resonated with me. I mean, if everybody is doing the same thing, maybe it's wise to try something different."

"That is a beautiful story," he agreed. "It shows that there are different ways to God," he said. "Just like your hand. It has four fingers and one thumb but they are all attached to one hand."

"Well, here is the train station," I announced. I steered the car to the side of the road and stopped. He looked at me with a pair of large brown eyes.

"I have something I would like to give you," he said.

He took off a necklace he was wearing around his neck and handed it to me.

"A rosary? Nah, I couldn't." I said.

"Not a rosary. Prayer beads. Please. Wear it around your neck. It will bring you good luck."

"Nah, you can keep it."

"It will allow me to grant you one wish," he said.

"I can have one wish?"

He nodded. Wow. Nobody had ever offered to grant me a wish before.

"But only if you put on this necklace. And know this, whatever you wish for, is guaranteed to come true. But you must say the wish aloud and with confidence. What do you wish for, my brother?"

I have to admit, as I put on the necklace, I got nervous. My first thought was to wish for 60 million dollars cash, but I hesitated. Hold on. There's gotta be a catch. My wish might be granted, for example, but then there might be some bullshit *Twilight Zone* fine print attached to it. I might have to live in a mental hospital, for example, or not be allowed to use the money, or something crappy like that. So I wished for something stupid and banal. Before I tell you what I wished for, let me ask you a question. Friend, if someone could grant you one wish, right now, what would you wish for? Say it aloud, right now!

I didn't have all day to answer him because the clock was ticking and his train would be arriving at the train station any second now.

"Well, what is your wish?" he asked.

"I wish for good health," I decided.

He nodded his head. "Ah, that is a wise choice, my friend. Wear this necklace always. Meditate and exercise daily. Avoid eating red meat. Your wish will come true."

With that, the holy man left my car and I never saw him again. I still wear the necklace and my health is good. Knock on wood.

-13-

FOURTH OF JULY

For most local residents, the annual Fourth of July parade which takes place in Santa Clarita is a big deal. The city hangs about 200 American flags on each side of Lyons Avenue and shuts down or re-routes traffic for a few hours.

The parade route itself spans a distance of only a few miles, yet this event draws a crowd of between 8,000 -10,000 people who enjoy the sun, watch the festivities, and wave at the participants. High school bands play, equestrians ride their horses, Cub Scouts pedal their bicycles while local dignitaries and beauty queens travel in classic cars or wave while being transported by modern convertibles.

True to his word, Larry's entry had made it in the parade. Someone had hoisted the piano on the back of a stake truck and Larry was pounding the keys, surrounded by four attractive "saloon girls" wearing high-heels and black fishnet stockings. Dressed in a frilly, white shirt, vest and bow tie, Larry looked like a barkeep from the Old West who seemed to be having a wonderful time.

My wife and I watched the spectacle from a grassy area on Orchard Village Road. When it was over, Roxy gave me a kiss goodbye and then we went our separate ways. She had things to do and I had agreed to help Larry schlep the piano back to Pine Mountain.

A short while later, I located Mike who had also agreed to help. By 12:30 p.m. the streets had turned back to normal, so with the song "Funkytown" blaring from my car radio and Mike sitting shotgun beside me, I drove slowly down Lyons Avenue towards the freeway. I had enlisted Mike's assistance with the piano because I feared getting that heavy beast back into Larry's house might prove to be a lot harder than getting it out. So we were following behind Larry's white Suburban and his U-Haul trailer.

"I think that there should really be a sequel song to this one," said Mike.

"Huh? I muttered. "What are you talking about?"

"Just saying, there ought to be a sequel song about needing a ride BACK from 'Funkytown.'"

"Oh that, I wasn't really paying attention."

"Holy shit," Mike yelled. "There's a cop!"

Mike's sudden announcement caused him to drop his head and for me to immediately slow down. Mike seemed to get nervous over every little thing, and I sometimes wondered if Mike was an escaped felon.

"Why is it whenever we see a police car," Mike observed. "That we drive like we have ten kilos of cocaine and a stolen baby in the car?"

"Why is it that you have to scare the shit out of me," I responded.

We drove for a little while and I asked Mike about the beautiful Swedish lady we had met while door-knocking.

"Hilda? I didn't tell you about her? I thought everybody knew. Oh, that's right, you got to the meeting late. That's when we started bagging Larry about Hitler and Charles Manson having girlfriends and him not."

"Okay, so what happened?"

"Well, at first she was really cool, and then she kinda turned creepy," Mike said. "When I went over there that night, she was STILL wearing her bikini, and she said, 'Let's go swimming.'"

I had to slow down for a stoplight but looked over. "Then what happened?"

Mike continued. "I told her that I didn't have any swimming trunks, and she pulled out a pair of Speedo's that were waay too small. But I put them on anyway and dude it made my tiny penis look enormous."

"Okay, so did anything happen?" I asked.

"Hell, yeah! She fucked my brains out," he said, "Sex with her was off the frickin' chain!"

"I mean, did you list her house?" I asked.

"Oh, that. No, she's not ready to sell yet."

"Ah ha," I murmured. "So why did you say things turned creepy?"

"I saw her maybe a couple-dozen times after that and she was cool. One night she didn't wear any underwear under her mini-skirt, and we had sex outdoors! Another time I tied her up to her bed and blindfolded her. We had sex at a spa, sex in my car, but the truth is, we had nothing else. We just had sex and more sex and then I would leave. So I finally told her, 'Hey, we need to talk.' I swear, dude, I sounded like a chick. I said, 'Look Hilda, I want to get married and have kids some day and I don't think this is gonna work out. I think that we should stop seeing each other.'"

"What did she say?"

"Hilda didn't say anything. She just got all sad and started to cry."

"That's a woman for you," I said.

"Yeah, so one morning I'm pulling out of my driveway," he continued. "And I see this red Honda Civic parked across the street. At first, I didn't think anything of it, but then I realized who it was. It was HILDA! She had her little girl in the car, and they were following me!"

"No way! Did you bust her on it?"

"Yes! I stopped at the next stop sign, got out of my car and yelled, 'What the fuck are you doing? Why are you following me?"

"What did she say?"

"Nothing. She just took off. But every once in a while, I get this creepy feeling that she's still following me."

A sexy woman following you. Hmm. Things could be A LOT worse, I thought to myself.

We had just gotten onto the 5 Freeway. In front of us, a few car lengths ahead, Larry put pedal to the metal to gain some distance. Suddenly, Larry's Suburban with rented trailer hit a bump and almost in slow motion the following things happened in this exact order:

The trailer jumped about three feet off the ground.

The trailer doors flung wide open.

The piano bounced out of the trailer and rolled out onto

the next lane of the freeway, waiting, waiting, until...

smash! A passing 18 wheeler collided with Larry's piano.

Bits of the oak wood flew out from the bottom of the truck like slush as a second passing big-rig crushed it.

I pulled over to the shoulder of the freeway and stopped the car.

"Holy shit-balls!" Mike exclaimed. "Did you see that?!"

Likewise, Larry had pulled the Suburban over to the side of the road, stopped the car and jumped out.

"No, no, no!" he wailed. "I can't believe this!"

Tears were running down his face, but it was too late to do anything. The piano that had taken him years to painstakingly put together was now nothing but a bunch of oak kindling, busted black keys and old piano wires. Guess he might need a ride back from Funkytown after all, I thought. But how could he forget to do something so simple, like properly tie up the piano? Did he assume someone else did it? Was he in such a hurry that he never checked it?

Mike exclaimed. "Damn, I wish I would have videoed that shit! That would have been epic on YouTube!"

Then I realized something basic. Something so simple about Kelly and the pony I could almost kick myself. An epic video. Why hadn't I thought of this before?

"Mike, stay here with Larry? I've got to go back to the office and check something out," I said. "I just thought of something I've got to do."

"Sure thing. Come here, you idiot," Mike said consoling Larry. "Hey, one of my friends had a baby today and another got a puppy. I think we all know which one I'm going to visit. Come on. Wanna go and see a puppy? Come on, buck up, Larry."

* * *

Instead of returning to the office, I drove 20 miles east to Kelly's old house in Agua Dulce where Mr. Juan Ortega was pulling weeds. He looked up and smiled as I pulled to a stop and got out of my car.

"Good to see you, Mr. Bob," he said while extending his hand.

"Likewise, it's good to see you Juan," I said warmly. "Happy Fourth of July."

Juan always seemed like such a humble soul, I sometimes worried he might be putting on an act. Like, what if he was just pretending not to be as good any everyone else? Then I was really screwed.

"Mister Bob, would you like to come inside and see what

we've done with the house?" he asked.

"Por supuesto," (Of course) I answered.

Hard-working Juan proudly showed me all the improvements he had made. Looking out from his kitchen window, he explained how he had rebuilt the entire roof, cleaned out all the mud, and had even built a small retaining wall behind the house where a gardener's shed was now standing. A cement culvert had been dug to divert any water coming down from the hillside and it all looked like it was done to code and appeared very professional.

"Nice job," I said.

"This cost a lot of money. Have you been able to talk to the seller?" he asked.

"About what?" I said.

"About the things I lost in the flood. The inundation that she failed to disclose to me. This disaster has cost me over $28,000. I have all my receipts here."

He opened a drawer and pulled out a massive amount of paperwork to prove his case, and I used my cell phone to take pictures of the major bills. The roof work alone was over $18,000.

"Well, I have some good news and bad news," I said and I showed him a copy of the flooding disclosure. "This is your signature, here, isn't it Juan?"

He nodded.

"This is obviously Kelly's signature. So you both signed this document, which states that the house does get flooded when it rains. So you can't say she didn't warn you because she DID disclose the flooding problem to you. It says it right here. There is nothing you can do about it."

Juan reminded me of Larry seeing his piano decimated on the freeway. I really thought he was going to cry.

"Look Juan, here is what I am willing to do. I will ask Kelly to drop her request that you pay her the $24,000 for the pony, but I will only do this on one condition: that win or lose, you do not come after and sue me afterwards. Would that work out for you?"

"Yes, Mister Bob, please. I can't promise but I don't want to sue you. You have been very fair to me, however, I did have to pay a lot of money to fix all of this."

"I understand. Shake on it?"

With a pump of hands, skin on skin, our deal was finalized.

Agreed, it wasn't worth the paper it was written on, but at least with Juan it meant something.

-14-

FAR WORSE NIGHTMARES

Youtube is probably one of the greatest places for videos. It's also one of the few places where you will find people arguing about religion in the comments of a snowboarding video. The back and forth arguing is sometimes humorous but often just horrendous.

Likewise, the bickering before the Friday morning meeting started got bad until I asked the gang to change the subject. They were talking about Kelly and the pony and what I should do. "Look, there are folks who have suffered FAR worse real estate nightmares– and people who have experienced far worse horror stories in general," I said, "but things will work out. I just have to stay positive, right?" Nobody said a word, so I continued. "Look, a friend of mine has a 26 year-old daughter named Lily who works as a Zumba instructor. One day, she woke up and discovered she couldn't move. She could not feel her hands or legs: her entire body was paralyzed.

Lily was rushed to the hospital where doctors diagnosed

her with a rare blood disease that attacks the nerve cells. At age 26, Lily may be paralyzed for the rest of her life. Horrible, isn't it? But Lily was released from the hospital, and I am told that she is doing much better at home. She is walking and taking one step at a time." I looked around the conference room. "So, bad things can happen to good people but good people make the best of things and move on. Anyone else have a nightmare they would like to share?"

"I have a relative nightmare," said Larry.

"A relative nightmare?" Mike questioned.

"Yeah," Larry responded. "Like, who needs Google when you have a brother-in-law who knows it all? We all have experienced that kind of nightmare, haven't we?"

"Here's another story. I have a friend named Carlos," I said. "At age 49, Carlos suffered a massive stroke that left half his body paralyzed. Doctors at Cedar Sinai Medical Center told Carlos he had two months left to live and he should get all his affairs in order.

When Carlos was wheeled into my office, I estimated that he had two weeks to live because he looked as gaunt and pale as a Holocaust survivor. Carlos had paid off his house and wanted to sign a deed to leave his property to his 20 year old son. Carlos feared that his son might have a problem with probate after he passed away, and if Carlos didn't pass away, well, at least the house was paid off, so there wouldn't be a house payment to worry about.

I told Carlos, 'I spoke to the lady at escrow and asked her to draw up two deeds for you. One is for what you have asked for, and the other is for what I would recommend: a quitclaim deed that deeds the property to both you and your son, because you never know. A miracle might happen, and if it does, what if your son refuses to give the property back to you?' He said, 'Thank you, Mr. Bob, but that would NEVER happen. I mean, I know how Anglo families can be cold and heartless to their parents, but we Latin people are different. If I cannot trust my son, who can I trust? I just want to give him the house and be done with it. I am also giving him $55,000, as well as my auto-repair business. I want him to have everything. I am ready to meet my maker.'

That was the last I saw of skinny, emaciated Carlos.

At least for two years.

Because one day, two years later, Carlos walked into my office. Incredibly, he DID experience a miracle cure! He went from weighing under 120 pounds to over 200 pounds and now looked as fit as a fiddle.

Unfortunately, the story he told was not a happy one.

'Mr. Bob', he said, 'I just got out of jail.'

'What?' I exclaimed. I couldn't believe it.

'Yes, and I should have listened to you because you were right, but I was too stubborn to believe you.'

'What are you talking about? What happened?'

'A miracle. God cured me. Unfortunately, my son and his new girlfriend got tired of me. His new girlfriend claimed that I was costing them a fortune in food and water and demanded that I move out of the main house. They moved all my things to the detached garage with no heating or air conditioning.'

'That is so sad!' I exclaimed.

'It gets worse. When I was 100 percent cured, my son's girlfriend insisted that I find a job or she would have me evicted. So not wanting to be homeless, I worked with my brother fixing roofs. One day when I was working, she entered my room and placed a loaded pistol under my bed in the garage where I stayed. Then, when I came home, I was relaxing, drinking a beer, when the police came.'

'Why?'

'She called and claimed that I had threatened her with a gun. When the police searched my place, they found the weapon, handcuffed me, and threw me in jail. Because it was the Labor Day holiday, I spent three days locked up in County Jail. When I finally got released, all of my possessions had been thrown over the fence, and I was locked out of my own house. Or garage as it may be.'

'That is terrible,' I said.

'I was wondering if you knew of a lawyer who could help me,' he said. 'I want to get my property back.'

To make a long story short, Carlos filed a lawsuit against his son and explained to the judge what had happened. The son agreed to give Carlos $35,000 in cash, but Carlos refused to accept a single penny. He wanted the house back or nothing, and his son refused to give it to him.

Unfortunately, because Carlos had willingly deeded the property to his son, Carlos lost the case and has NOT spoken to his son or seen his grandchildren ever since."

"What a fucking depressing story!" Larry complained.

"Yeah," Mike agreed. "Talk about a buzz-kill."

"Hey, the story of Carlos reminds us that miracles can and do happen," I said. "Carlos is still alive. He has a job with his brother. A roof over his head. Good health."

"Is this some kind of a downer pep-talk?"

"Don't you get it?" Sandy Johnson explained. "Bob is trying to keep a positive attitude about his upcoming hearing."

"When is your hearing?" Mike asked.

"A week from today." I answered.

"Good luck," Larry said.

Everyone looked at me.

It was at that moment that I realized, that about 50% of the time, when people wish you "good luck" it really means, "poor bastard."

-15-

A Not so Grand Finale

If my life became a motion picture, there would probably be a famous, handsome actor playing my role; or at least not someone as ugly as me. There would be an exciting or compelling court-room showdown between two actors, like when Jack Nickolson screamed, "You can't handle the truth!" in the movie *A Few Good Men*.

But real life is different. The truth is often messier and less dramatic than fiction. Or at least for me. Plus things can happen rather anti-climatically too.

I have been to small-claims court only once before, for example, and my experience there was so unbelievable, it would NEVER make it into a movie. Here is what happened:

I was representing a Hispanic buyer who didn't speak much English. He and his wife were attempting to get their earnest money deposit back from the seller, an Asian lady, who had wanted to keep it.

It was now the listing agent's turn to explain why the seller, Mrs. Chin, deserved to keep the $3,000 earnest money.

At that very moment, a cell phone rang in court and the listing agent answered it. Then he continued his conversation and actually turned and began walking out of court. About halfway out the door, he stopped, turned to the judge and said, "I'm sorry, but I have to leave. I have an important meeting," and he actually left the building.

We were all stunned.

The judge was not amused. He yelled, "Bailiff, bring him back in here!"

A few minutes later, the well-dressed listing agent returned, and stood there sheepishly as the judge publicly reprimanded him like a father might scold a child. The judge then ruled in my clients' favor.

Later, I was in my car getting ready to leave and had just turned the key in the ignition when someone KNOCKED on my car window. I practically jumped through the ceiling. Standing there was Mrs. Chin, motioning me to roll down my car window, so I complied.

"I am so sorry about what happened in the court room," she apologized. "Listing agent is number one in his company, but I don't like him. I don't understand why he did what he did. Please, here is a personal check for the buyers. Can you give it to them for me?"

"Yes, of course."

Up close, dark-rings made Mrs. Chin's tired eyes resemble an Asian raccoon.

"I own another house that I would like to sell," she said. "I would be honored if you would list it for me."

Really? Inside my brain started to do cartwheels. I was thinking, me? Me? She wants ME to list her house and not the number one agent? But outwardly, I displayed a benign smile. "Yes, of course, I would be happy to list it for you."

Later, I can remember passing a bus bench and seeing black teeth and a moustache painted on the listing agent's face. Looking good, I had thought. Looking REAL good.

Bottom-line: I ended up listing Mrs. Chin's house and bringing the buyer for it myself too. Too unbelievable, perhaps for a movie. But it did happen in real life.

* * *

Now back to my nightmare and how everything ended.

I decided to go balls out on offense and confront Kelly's attorney in person. My strategy was to lay everything on the line. My best defense, I decided, was to be proactive.

I drove to his law office, parked my car, and stepped towards the four-story office building. Unlike my work-place, this sleek, newer edifice was located on Valencia Blvd near the City Hall. I took the elevator to the fourth floor, exited and moved down the hallway. My heart was pounding as I noticed an expensive-looking sign reading: James & Associates Law Firm.

Upon entering the office, Meghan, an attractive receptionist looked up at me. Standing next to her was a man wearing silver, thin-rimmed glasses who casually turned his head up and I recognized him as Andy James, Kelly's attorney.

"Hi, Mr. James?" I said. "My name is Bob Boog, do you have a moment?"

He stared at me carefully.

"Is this going to take long?"

"Ten minutes," I said.

"Follow me."

We went back to his private office, where he closed the door behind and offered me a seat. Hanging on one wall was his undergraduate degree from Harvard. I stared at it in awe, obviously impressed.

"Did you go to college?" he asked me.

"Yes, UCLA."

"What was your major?"

"I got my BA in English."

"Ahh," he said somewhat condescendingly. "Well, did you get a date for the arbitration hearing?"

"Not exactly," I explained.

"What do you mean, 'not exactly'? What are you doing here?"

"You see, I think there's been a big mistake. But one that can be corrected."

"A mistake?" his face soured at my word choice.

"Yes, this matter is really between Kelly and the buyer. Not me."

"I don't follow you."

"Well, if I go to arbitration I am going to insist that the buyer be there with me to verify that there was an agreement to purchase the pony. You wouldn't object to that, would you?"

"No, of course not."

"See, that's where the shit hits the fan. Because while the buyer is sitting there, he's going to learn that Kelly fraudulently switched the pony on him."

"Oh, so now you are accusing my client of fraud?"

"Yes, and I can prove it too."

I retrieved my cell phone from my shirt pocket and played Kelly's voice message for him. The phrase "You made me buy a pony for those fucking Mexicans" rang out loud and clear.

Andy blushed.

"This does NOT prove that she did anything fraudulent," he argued.

"Maybe not, but Kelly couldn't step onto the property by herself, correct? There was a restraining order in effect against her."

"What's your point?"

"My point is that Kelly contacted the Sheriff's Department, and they helped her remove the pony from the premises. In fact, I contacted the Sheriff's Department and, believe it or not, they actually keep records of such things."

"So? This still doesn't prove anything," he said. "Your appraisal came in short by $24,000 so she left them a pony. It didn't matter whether or not it was the same pony. It just had to be worth $24,000, right?"

"Well, I don't know about that. The buyers only agreed to do the deal because they have a 10 year old daughter who loved that particular pony."

"Kelly left them with a pony," he stated firmly.

"But it was not the same pony that was promised to them. Kelly can claim that she didn't switch the pony, but once the buyer views my records from the Sheriff's Department and hears the voice message she left me, the buyer may not agree with you. I mean he might, but I doubt it."

"What can the buyer do?" he scoffed. "He can't do anything, and you know it."

"Not true. The buyer could claim that he was tricked. He was promised one thing but given another and therefore, the entire sale transaction was based on fraud. In fact, he could demand ALL of his money back plus damages. Let's see, $224,000, that's what he paid for the property. Plus, damages in fraud cases can be ten times the amount, can't they? Over two million dollars? Are you sure you still want to go to arbitration with me?"

Andy's face turned red. "You had the duty to create a note and deed of trust for that transaction prior to the closing and you failed to execute your duties that are found under the California Civil Code."

"Oh, that may be true," I admitted, "but I was following section 1750 of the California Civil Code. This section, I believe, might pre-date yours because it deals specifically with selling horses. See, back in the Old West, people used to buy and sell horses all the time. According to this statute, a person selling a horse or pony must create a Bill of Sale first before the actual sale takes place, and this Bill of Sale must be notarized."

Andy gave me a deer in the headlights expression.

"Obviously, you never sold a horse before," I said. "But a Bill of Sale discourages a seller from showing a buyer a healthy animal but then later delivering a damaged, inferior, or lame one."

"I know what a bill of sale is."

The door suddenly popped open and the attractive receptionist stepped in, saw me and stopped. "Oh, I'm sorry Mr. James, but Mrs. Rudolph is waiting for you."

I noticed a bead of sweat trickling down Andy's forehead.

"Give me another minute, Meghan," Andy said.

Meghan instantly departed.

"Where were we?" Andy said.

"Two weeks before closing escrow, the appraisal came in low. So for 14 days I asked Kelly to come to my office with her vet records so I could create a Bill of Sale, and she refused. Why? Because maybe she decided that her pony was her pet. Her baby. Like one of her kitty-cats. And she hadn't yet bought a second pony. That's why she claims that I made her buy a pony for the buyers."

Andy stared at me. "You can't prove any of this."

"You're right. But I bet I could subpoena the place where Kelly purchased the pony," I bluffed. "She used to board her pony there before she bought the house and I believe she boards it there now. Plus, there is the matter of the State Board of Equalization too."

"What are you talking about?"

At this point, I have to admit, Andy's Harvard education didn't make me respect him more. It sort of made me respect Harvard a little less.

"The sales tax? In California, when you purchase a soda at the local 7-Eleven convenience store, you will pay a sales tax, won't you? When I told Kelly a sales tax would apply to the sale of the pony, she didn't want to hear about it. And I told her she could pay it up front, and have me add it to the loan, but she said 'no'. I think it's another reason why she didn't want to come by my office. Because she didn't want to pay that tax."

"What is it you are proposing?" Andy demanded.

"Do you have a copy of the counter offer that Kelly signed?" I asked. Before he could answer, I passed him a photocopy that I had made.

Andy glanced at it as I continued.

"In this counter, Kelly agreed to repair the roof but never did, and for the past year, whenever it rained, the house flooded. Just the other day it rained just a little bit, but it caused a significant amount of damage to the buyer's property. I went to their house and took pictures with my cell phone so you can see."

I showed Andy several pictures I had taken of Juan's house. The hole in the kitchen ceiling, the massive amount of mud, the walls with blue-green mold, the damaged TV, etc. The house looked like a beach littered with debris after a big storm.

"Holy shit."

"Here are some of his receipts."

"Mr. Ortega said that he had to change the pitch of the roof to fix it properly, and dig a special channel to drain the water that was not disclosed to him. He said it cost around $28,000 not including his pain and suffering."

"How much money are we talking about?"

Plus, they had to stay at a hotel for a week while repairs were made. It was a big mess, but like I said, he still does not know one thing about the pony, so I'm thinking $24,000 would do."

"$24,000. How convenient."

"If Kelly agrees to cancel the agreement for him to buy the pony, he will drop any and all future litigation against her too."

"Okay, but this still doesn't let you off the hook," Andy warned. "You are still being held responsible for the condition of the property and the $17,000 worth of damages."

"How so?"

"You were responsible for renting the house to the Curstons."

"Not true."

"Not true? Your signature is on the management agreement, right here. This is your signature, isn't it?"

Andy pulled out the rental form and showed it to me. Yep. There it was, my signature, clear as a bell.

"That is your signature, isn't it?"

"Yes."

"I rest my case," he said.

"Not so fast. Kelly found those tenants, not me."

"Oh, so now you are saying that she found the Curstons?"

"Yes," I explained. "The Curstons were members of her church and after I ran their credit I had advised Kelly not to rent to them. That's why she never paid me a penny for my services. She found the tenants and rented to them on her own. Ask her. Even the Curstons will verify it, and so will Kelly's youth pastor."

"You signed this agreement, so I don't have to ask anybody anything." Andy shook his head. "See, you can't prove that you were NOT responsible, that's your problem."

"That's not exactly true," I said and I pulled out my cell phone and played the brief video clip that I had taken the day Pastor Jim and I had gone there. On the video Cynthia told Pastor Jim:

"'We struck a deal with the owner by ourselves and then Mr. Bob Boog here had to go and mess the whole thing up. My mother would have OWNED this place if it wasn't for him.'"

Andy didn't say anything, so I turned off the video.

"I mean she does say, 'We struck a deal with the owner and then Mr. Bob Boog had to go and mess the whole thing up,'" I prodded.

He grinned. "The Curstons will never testify for you."

"Oh that's for sure," I admitted "But I bet I could bring that Christian minister to testify on my behalf. If we are all standing in front of a judge, who do you think he or she will find more believable? Kelly, me, or the Christian minister?"

"I guess we will find out, won't we?" Andy responded. He paused to lift his face toward me as he did a minute ago, with the same dead-cool air, as if knowing he would be able to defeat me somehow.

Shit. I thought to myself. Why isn't he giving up now?

"Well, keep this in mind," I reminded, "Kelly is a woman who was so mentally unstable that she had a restraining order filed against her. A woman who was so in love with her pony that she refused to lawfully sign the Bill of Sale and leave it for the buyers when she had agreed to do so. A woman who agreed to fix the roof but never did. She's not exactly reliable. Who knows what she's going to say in front of a judge?"

"I will see you in arbitration," Andy stated. He gave me his best bad dog look again.

"One last thing, a reputation for professionalism is important to me," I said. "I have worked in real estate for 30 years and have never been sued."

"So?"

"I understand that you have never lost a case."

"Big deal. There's always a first time."

"Well, let me ask you a question, what will all your Twitter and Facebook friends think once they learn that you lost a case? And not only did you lose it, it wasn't to some fancy Beverly Hills lawyer, but to a lousy real estate agent?"

Andy clenched his jaw.

"Okay, I gave you a chance," I shrugged.

I got up, moved to the door and stopped, "My attorney will contact you about the hearing date. We do have someone set up."

The truth is that I was lying out of my ass. I did not have a lawyer. I did not have an arbitrator. I didn't have a date. I didn't have two cents in the bank. I had nothing but confidence. Even that was dwindling.

I reached for the doorknob and opened the door.

"Wait," he said. "Wait." He sounded desperate so I stopped and slowly turned.

In real estate, there is a saying which goes: He who speaks first, loses.

I did not utter a word. I just gave my best teenage, bored impression. The same one I had given the hillbillies.

He stared at me sulkily, looking me over, then briefly closed his eyes. "You're right," he admitted. "No judge would ever believe her. She is nuttier than my nutsack."

"Then, I will get something from you in writing?" I said.

He threw a hand up in disgust.

"I will send you a cancellation in the mail," he promised. "Give me two days."

With that, I stepped towards him casually and the two of us shook hands.

As I walked outside, it was another beautiful sunny day in Santa Clarita, California. The sky was blue and it had to be close to 80 degrees out, but I kept thinking back to when I was a kid ice skating with my mother on a frozen lake in Minnesota. I thought about my mom telling me about the first time my little hand had left hers. She said that I had the biggest grin on my face because though I was unable to walk on my own, I could skate and glide freely on the ice on my own. She said I was the most determined kid she ever knew, and that it was a good thing too.

I now felt elated but I also had the awkward feeling you get when you leave a store without buying anything and all you can think is, "Dude, act natural. You have been found innocent!"

-16-

FINAL THOUGHTS

True to his word, I received formal notification the arbitration hearing had been dropped. Whew! I breathed a sigh of relief.

A few days after receiving the letter, I parked my car in front of a non-descriptive, one-story bungalow located off Lyons Avenue, where the sign on the wooden door reads: "Pastor Jim – Christian Counselor."

I carried a box of fresh-baked cookies I had picked up at a Vons grocery store. Every Thursday, Pastor Jim serves a free lunch to anybody who wants to show up. It's mostly a ragtag group of retired men who break bread and share stories around a large wooden table and after lunch they have a Bible study.

I entered the living room and stepped to the kitchen where I found Pastor Jim preparing some pasta.

"Well, well, well, look who the cat dragged in," he said with a smile.

"I brought you some cookies," I announced.

"I see that. Can you stay for lunch? We'd love to have you."

"Nah, I've got to watch my girlish figure," I joked. "Plus I've got to get back to work," I motioned my head in the general direction of my office.

"Hey, I just wanted you to know that everything worked out like you said," I told him. "So I wanted to say thank you."

"Bob, it was never about you," Pastor Jim said. "Believe it or not, you were acting as God's real estate agent."

Ha, I thought to myself. I can just imagine putting that on my business cards.

"Yeah, well, whatever, thank you for all of your help."

"Bob, whether you believe me or not; prayer can work wonders," he said. "You ought to try it some time."

"Yes, but in this case it was also important to know about needing a bill of sale," I said.

"By the way," he asked. "How did you know that selling the pony would involve a bill of sale?"

"It's pretty commonplace when a property doesn't appraise at full value. Many buyers will offer to purchase a stove, or furniture or whatever, so a bill of sale is used. The first one I ever did, the seller came back to me to complain that he got in trouble with the State Board of Equalization because he failed to pay the sales tax. So I knew Kelly would have to sign one and pay the tax. I did have to Google the correct California Civil Code Section, though."

"Well, you did a great job, and you really got those tenants to move out?" he stated more than questioned.

"Yup."

"And they didn't destroy the place?"

"Nope."

"Now that is a miracle," he laughed.

We shook hands and he gave me a hug.

As I left, I heard someone ask Pastor Jim, "Who was that guy?"

Pastor Jim answered, "That was Bob Boog, the real estate broker. He told me one of the weirdest, amazing but true real estate stories I have ever heard."

I left the house, jumped in my car and drove away.

I didn't go far because I had to stop at the stoplight on Lyons, and as I did, I noticed Mike Mitchell in his late model Toyota racing by. I was about to honk, but he sped past too quickly. About fifteen seconds later, I noticed an attractive, blonde woman with a determined look on her face following behind Mike.

She was driving a red Honda Civic and had a small child with her.

Strange, but true.

This has been an actual part of my life. As mentioned before, it's "based on a true story" which means it happened more or less like this, but with uglier people.

Thanks for reading it. Good day or good night, wherever you are.

Oh, okay, thanks for the tip.

I was actually planning on letting the bed bugs bite, but good call.

THE END

Here is a preview of Bob's next book
scheduled for November 2015

THE REAL ESTATE
ROOKIE

During the early 1980's, the Santa Clarita Valley, or SCV as it is commonly referred to, was pretty much the same as it is now – except that there was only about 50,000 people living here. (Nowadays there are about 250,000.) At that time of course, cell phones had not been invented, few people were vegans, Ronald Reagan was president and Michael Jackson was the top musical star. Back then, *Space Invaders, Pac Man, Frogger and Asteroids* were the big video games.

The SCV had less than 100,000 residents (we now have close to 300,000) there was no regional shopping mall and no place to really meet women, except for Genesis, the discotheque inside the local bowling alley, my friends commonly referred to as "Genitals".

At that time, I was in my early 20s, single, with a full-head of hair and my father was the broker of our real estate company. Back then our office consisted of my dad and mom, myself, an agent name Jim Watkins, (Larry's older brother) Sandy Johnson and her mother Joyce.

Larry's brother Jim looked exactly like Jim Carey with a mullet and while Joyce's pleasant, plump face somewhat resembled her daughter Sandy. It was weird because though they both shared blonde hair and blue eyes, Joyce always walked around with a bitter expression on her face – like she had just taken a bite from a sour lemon.

I was sitting in the conference room of our real estate company waiting for the weekly meeting to start, and Jim was killing time by making observations.

"Hey, have you ever thought about the song, *Row, Row, Row Your Boat?*" Jim continued.

"Um, not really. Why?" I asked.

"To me, it just doesn't make any sense. By definition, a stream is smaller than a river. And if a rowboat is heading down a stream, it shouldn't really need to be rowed, right? So imagine that someone is actually inside a heavy rowboat in a small body of water rowing, and saying that 'life is but a dream.' It just doesn't make any sense!"

"It's a British song," I told him, "so it probably makes sense to them. Here is something that I wonder about: you know how Brits always say, 'bloody hell,' or 'bloody this,' or 'bloody that?' What do they say when there is actually some blood on something?"

"I never thought about that," Jim marveled.

"Don't get him started," Joyce warned me. She then turned to Jim and said, "There's an old saying you should learn that goes like this: everything happens for a reason. Sometimes the reason is that you're stupid."

Oohh. Fighting words.

"At least I'm not ugly," Jim countered. "Like you."

"I'm not ugly."

"Oh yes, you are. You are so ugly, I bet your pillow cries at night."

Joyce rolled her eyes. "Is that the best you've got?"

"Okay, you're so ugly, that when you look in the mirror your reflection ducks."

"Ha, ha. That's so funny, I forgot to laugh."

"Okay, You're so ugly that you have to get your vibrator drunk before it will sleep with you."

Before she could respond, my dad entered the conference room and put a stop to the chaos.

Paul Boog, my dad, is a short guy in his late 50's who many people think looks like Paul Newman. Some people believe my dad is Jewish because of his attention to detail and frugalness. A slender man who exercises daily, Paul entered the room burdened with a box of what I assumed were training materials.

"Children, children, come on, let's behave now," he said. "We've got some work to do, plus I've got a very important announcement to make."

Everyone looked up at my dad.

"Last year, there was an agent named Jenny Getz who sold 65 homes in her first year in real estate."

Jim nodded his head as if to say, "not bad."

"She was awarded the 'Rookie of the Year' award in the state of Washington. And today, she is joining our firm. So without further ado, I would like to present to you, Ms. Jenny Getz."

At 36 years old, Jenny entered the conference room wearing a dress and high heel pumps. A pretty blonde who stood about 5'2" Jenny's face had the substance of maturity, intelligence and purpose. She took a moment to gaze around the room and her eyes caught my attention.

"Tell us a little bit about yourself," my dad said.

"My name is Jenny Getz," she said in a southern accent. "I am originally from Tennessee so folks say that I talk with an accent. I am married and have two small children, ages 6 and 7. My husband works as a truck driver, and yes, last year I was named the Rookie of the Year in the state of Washington. I am excited to join your team here in sunny Santa Clarita, California and am looking forward to meeting you all personally."

With that, we all applauded. Except, for Jim, who stood up and applauded, with an even extra bit of enthusiasm, I might add.

"Hopefully Jenny will be able to share her sales experiences with you," my Dad said.

I noticed Jenny's eyes had not stopped looking at me.

I nodded.

With the introduction over, my dad got into opening the box.

"Inside this box is the latest in sales technology," said my dad.

"What is it?" Jim asked.

My dad removed the Styrofoam packaging to reveal a contraption that looked sleek and ultra-modern.

"This machine is the latest bit of real estate technology," he repeated.

"What's it called?"

"A facsimile machine. Some people call it a 'fax machine'"

"Fax machine?" Jim asked. "What does that do?"

"With this machine, we will be able to send pictures of homes anywhere over a telephone wire."

"Wow. That is amazing!" Jim said excitedly.

"Is he always this enthusiastic?" Jenny asked, looking over at me.

"Yep," I nodded my head and smiled. "Always."

LOOK FOR 'THE REAL ESTATE ROOKIE"

COMING OUT NOVEMBER 2015

Made in the USA
Lexington, KY
19 December 2016